also by the editors at america's test kitchen

The New Essentials Cookbook

Dinner Illustrated

Cooking at Home with Bridget and Julia

The Complete Slow Cooker

The Complete Make-Ahead Cookbook

The Complete Mediterranean Cookbook

The Complete Vegetarian Cookbook

The Complete Cooking for Two Cookbook

Just Add Sauce

How to Roast Everything

Nutritious Delicious

What Good Cooks Know

Cook's Science

The Science of Good Cooking

The Perfect Cake

The Perfect Cookie

Bread Illustrated

Master of the Grill

Kitchen Smarts

Kitchen Hacks

100 Recipes: The Absolute Best Ways to Make the True Essentials

The New Family Cookbook

The America's Test Kitchen Cooking School Cookbook

The Cook's Illustrated Meat Book

The Cook's Illustrated Baking Book

The Cook's Illustrated Cookbook

The America's Test Kitchen Family Baking Book

The Best of America's Test Kitchen (2007–2019 Editions)

The Complete America's Test Kitchen TV Show Cookbook 2001–2019

Sous Vide for Everybody

Multicooker Perfection

Food Processor Perfection

Pressure Cooker Perfection

Vegan for Everybody

Naturally Sweet

Foolproof Preserving

Paleo Perfected

The How Can It Be Gluten-Free Cookbook: Volume 2

The How Can It Be Gluten-Free Cookbook

The Best Mexican Recipes

Slow Cooker Revolution Volume 2: The Easy-Prep Edition

Slow Cooker Revolution

The Six-Ingredient Solution

The America's Test Kitchen D.I.Y. Cookbook

the cook's illustrated all-time best series

All-Time Best Brunch

All-Time Best Sunday Suppers

All-Time Best Holiday Entertaining

All-Time Best Appetizers

All-Time Best Soups

cook's country titles

One-Pan Wonders

Cook It in Cast Iron

Cook's Country Eats Local

The Complete Cook's Country TV Show Cookbook

for a full listing of all our books

CooksIllustrated.com

AmericasTestKitchen.com

dinners for two

COOK'S
ILLUSTRATED

all
time
best

dinners for two

the editors at
america's test kitchen

Library of Congress
Cataloging-in-Publication Data

Names: America's Test Kitchen (Firm), publisher.
Title: Cook's Illustrated all time best dinners for two / the editors at America's Test Kitchen.
Other titles: All time best dinners for two
Description: Boston, MA : America's Test Kitchen, [2018] | Includes index.
Identifiers: LCCN 2018008948 | ISBN 9781945256622
Subjects: LCSH: Cooking for two. | Dinners and dining. | LCGFT: Cookbooks.
Classification: LCC TX714 .C65479 2018 | DDC 641.5/612--dc23
LC record available at https://lccn.loc.gov/2018008948

AMERICA'S TEST KITCHEN
21 Drydock Ave, Boston, MA 02210

Manufactured in the United States of America

10 9 8 7 6 5 4 3 2

Distributed by Penguin Random House Publisher Services
Tel: 800.733.3000

Editorial Director, Books: Elizabeth Carduff
Executive Editor: Adam Kowit
Senior Managing Editor: Debra Hudak
Editorial Assistant: Alyssa Langer
Design Director, Books: Carole Goodman
Art Director: Lindsey Timko Chandler
Deputy Art Director: Allison Boales
Associate Art Director: Katie Barranger
Production Designer: Reinaldo Cruz
Photography Director: Julie Bozzo Cote
Photography Producer: Meredith Mulcahy
Senior Staff Photographer: Daniel J. van Ackere
Staff Photographer: Steve Klise
Additional Photography: Keller + Keller, Anthony Tieuli, and Carl Tremblay
Food Styling: Catrine Kelty, Chantal Lambeth, Marie Piraino, Elle Simone Scott, and Sally Staub
Photoshoot Kitchen Team:
    Manager: Timothy McQuinn
    Lead Test Cook: Daniel Cellucci
    Test Cook: Jessica Rudolph
    Assistant Test Cooks: Sarah Ewald, Eric Haessler, and Mady Nichas
Production Director: Guy Rochford
Senior Production Manager: Jessica Lindheimer Quirk
Production Manager: Christine Spanger
Imaging Manager: Lauren Robbins
Production and Imaging Specialists: Heather Dube, Dennis Noble, and Jessica Voas
Copy Editor: Elizabeth Wray Emery
Proofreader: Karen Wise
Indexer: Elizabeth Parson

Chief Creative Officer: Jack Bishop
Executive Editorial Directors: Julia Collin Davison and Bridget Lancaster

Pictured on front cover: Classic Lasagna (page 71)
Pictured on back cover (clockwise from bottom): Beef Stir-Fry with Bell Peppers and Black Pepper Sauce (page 58), Chili-Glazed Salmon with Bok Choy (page 112), Chicken Pot Pie (page 13), Herb-Rubbed Pork Tenderloin with Fennel and Artichokes (page 93)

contents

welcome to america's test kitchen

THIS BOOK HAS BEEN TESTED, WRITTEN, AND EDITED BY THE FOLKS at America's Test Kitchen. Located in Boston's Seaport District in the historic Innovation and Design Building, it features 15,000 square feet of kitchen space including photography and video studios. It is the home of *Cook's Illustrated* magazine and *Cook's Country* magazine and is the workday destination for more than 60 test cooks, editors, and cookware specialists. Our mission is to test recipes over and over again until we understand how and why they work and until we arrive at the best version.

We start the process of testing a recipe with a complete lack of preconceptions, which means that we accept no claim, no technique, and no recipe at face value. We simply assemble as many variations as possible, test a half-dozen of the most promising, and taste the results blind. We then construct our own recipe and continue to test it, varying ingredients, techniques, and cooking times until we reach a consensus. As we like to say in the test kitchen, "We make the mistakes so you don't have to." The result, we hope, is the best version of a particular recipe, but we realize that only you can be the final judge of our success (or failure). We use the same rigorous approach when we test equipment and taste ingredients.

All of this would not be possible without a belief that good cooking, much like good music, is based on a foundation of objective technique. Some people like spicy foods and others don't, but there is a right way to sauté, there is a best way to cook a pot roast, and there are measurable scientific principles involved in producing perfectly beaten, stable egg whites. Our ultimate goal is to investigate the fundamental principles of cooking to give you the techniques, tools, and ingredients you need to become a better cook. It is as simple as that.

To see what goes on behind the scenes at America's Test Kitchen, check out our social media channels for kitchen snapshots, exclusive content, video tips, and much more. You can watch us work (in our actual test kitchen) by tuning in to *America's Test Kitchen* or *Cook's Country* on public television or on our websites. Listen to test kitchen experts on public radio (Splendid-Table.org) to hear insights that illuminate the truth about real home cooking. Want to hone your cooking skills or finally learn how to bake—with an America's Test Kitchen test cook? Enroll in one of our online cooking classes. However you choose to visit us, we welcome you into our kitchen, where you can stand by our side as we test our way to the best recipes in America.

facebook.com/
AmericasTestKitchen

twitter.com/TestKitchen

youtube.com/
AmericasTestKitchen

instagram.com/TestKitchen

pinterest.com/TestKitchen

AmericasTestKitchen.com

CooksIllustrated.com

CooksCountry.com

OnlineCookingSchool.com

introduction

While we wish cooking dinner for two was as easy as cutting a recipe in half, in reality the process is a lot more complicated than simply scaling down the quantity of each ingredient. For this book, we took many of our favorite recipes and reengineered them from the ground up to yield two servings. Using clever tricks and techniques for everything from Skillet Eggplant Parmesan to Yankee Pot Roast, our goal was to ensure that our for-two versions were as stellar as their originals.

In this carefully curated collection, we made sure to include something for everyone. Want to skip the restaurant and have a date night at home? Enter elegant dishes such as Risotto Primavera or Steamed Mussels in White Wine with Parsley. You can try Pad Thai or Sichuan Orange Chicken with Broccoli when you are craving the bold flavors of takeout but don't want leftovers for days. If you're in a rush on a busy weeknight, no problem— nearly half of these meals take 45 minutes or less to prepare (times are provided for every recipe so you know the commitment beforehand). There are also plenty of meat-free options, from Asian Braised Tofu with Butternut Squash and Eggplant to Pasta with Roasted Cauliflower, Garlic, and Walnuts. Some recipes are full dinners that include a side dish (such as Parmesan and Basil-Stuffed Chicken with Roasted Carrots), while others are entrées (such as Herb-Crusted Beef Tenderloin) that can be paired with one of the 15 additional fuss-free, perfectly scaled side dishes provided in the appendix.

But this book doesn't just include recipes—we also share everything we've learned about cooking for two. In the following pages, we share our shopping strategies—such as how to buy just the right quantity of ingredients so extras don't go to waste—and how best to outfit your kitchen, as we recognize that storage and counter space can be more limited in for-two households. And no, you don't need all new equipment; we discovered that a loaf pan was the perfect vessel for baked brown rice, and that ramekins worked well for individual chicken pot pies.

Getting dinner for two on the table shouldn't be complicated, and our goal for this book was to make it as simple and foolproof as possible. From Beef Stroganoff (we use just one decadent 8-ounce filet mignon and cook the egg noodles directly in the sauce) to Baked Manicotti (we use no-boil lasagna noodles instead of fussy tube pasta and cleverly assemble it in a loaf pan), this collection truly represents the all-time best dinners for two.

for-two cooking:
your how-to guide

shopping smarter

how much do I need?

It can be tricky to figure out just how much of certain staple ingredients you need to purchase when you're cooking for only two—especially when you're trying to avoid food waste. Here's a cheat sheet of essential ingredients and the amounts needed to serve two. Memorize this and you won't overbuy at the supermarket.

- For roasted potatoes, you'll need just **1 pound of red potatoes**.

- A handful of leftover **green beans** is likely to go to waste; **8 ounces** is just enough for a simple side dish.

- Fresh spinach wilts down quite a bit, making it difficult to guess how much to buy. We recommend **5 ounces of fresh baby spinach** (or other salad greens) for an uncooked salad, or 10 ounces if the greens are being cooked.

- **Snap peas** are the perfect slightly sweet, crisp addition to salads and stir-fries; we suggest buying about **4 ounces**.

- Roasted **Brussels sprouts** make for a hearty, easy-to-prep side; **8 ounces** should be just enough.

- It can be difficult to determine just how much broccoli a head will yield before it's cut up. We recommend purchasing a **1-pound head of broccoli** (or cauliflower), which you can then cut into wedges before cooking.

continued on next page

Getting dinner for two people on the table shouldn't result in a refrigerator full of leftovers or a pantry overloaded with extraneous ingredients, but all too often this occurs because grocery stores are designed to entice shoppers to buy more than they need (thanks to buy-one-get-one sales, lower prices for bigger quantities, and everything packaged in "family-size" portions). It can seem impossible to shop for two without a lot of waste, but we've found a few simple ways to buy just what you need.

get creative in the produce section Produce often poses the biggest challenge when shopping for two. Stores sell carrots by the bunch, lettuce by the head, and grapes and cherries in bags of 2 pounds or more. You may have better luck in the organic section, where produce is often sold loose by the pound. (Local farmers' markets are good for this, too.) And many grocery stores have a salad bar, which is the perfect spot to grab ¼ cup of olives, ½ cup of chopped pepper, or a couple of handfuls of lettuce. Individually quick-frozen produce is often as good or better than what you can get fresh, and you can thaw only what you need.

take a number at the meat counter If you can buy your meat at a local butcher shop or at the supermarket meat counter, go for it. With everything packaged and priced to order, you can purchase just what you need, whether it's ½ pound of ground meatloaf mix for Classic Lasagna (page 71) or two chicken breasts for Chicken Piccata (page 20). And don't hesitate to buy frozen shrimp; you can defrost what you need in minutes under cold running water.

pay more per pound It's hard to turn down a good deal, and it can seem silly to buy a small package of meat when you could get twice as much for less per pound. However, the alternative is spending more money, buying more than you need, and likely throwing any extra away when it spoils before you can eat it all. Instead, look for six eggs instead of a dozen to make our Asparagus and Goat Cheese Frittata (page 159), a 4-ounce container of sour cream for Chicken Soft Tacos (page 36), or a package of just two pork chops for Glazed Grilled Pork Chops with Sweet Potatoes (page 80). You may pay more per pound or ounce, but you'll spend less overall and have only what you need, eliminating the risk of wasting any leftovers.

look for individually wrapped options Many items are available in single-serving packages that make it easy to use just a small amount and keep the rest sealed. Smaller containers of yogurt, applesauce, sliced fruit, precooked rice, and even milk can help you reduce waste.

be thoughtful when buying in bulk If you do want to buy in bulk to take advantage of lower prices, choose items that will keep well long-term. Frozen vegetables and fruits, and dried pasta, beans, and rice are all good to buy in bulk. And buying meat in bulk and freezing it in manageable portions can also be worthwhile.

make the most of bouillon and broth concentrates Dehydrated and concentrated forms of chicken, beef, and vegetable broth are shelf-stable and cost-effective (because you're not paying for the water), plus they last for up to two years once opened. Simply mix with water to make just as much broth as you need. We particularly like **Orrington Farms Vegan Chicken Flavored Broth Base and Seasoning** and **Better than Bouillon Roasted Beef Base.**

boxed wine is your ace in the hole Once opened, a bottle of wine is usable for only about a week. But boxed wine has an airtight inner bag that prevents exposure to oxygen even after the box is opened, so the wine lasts up to one month.

reach for no-prep aromatics Many savory recipes call for onion or garlic. To save time on shopping and prep, we've found easy alternatives to both. An equal amount of store-bought frozen chopped onions can be used in place of chopped fresh onions in any recipe. You can also chop extra onion and freeze it in a zipper-lock bag to have on hand. And if you don't have fresh garlic, you can swap ¾ teaspoon granulated garlic for 1 teaspoon minced fresh garlic.

use shallots instead of onions Onions add great aromatic flavor to recipes, but a single onion is often too much for a recipe for two. To avoid forgotten onion halves going bad at the back of your fridge, you can swap them for shallots, another allium that offers similar flavor in a much smaller package—a single shallot will yield just a few tablespoons when minced.

use dried herbs (sometimes) Fresh herbs have a very short shelf life, and when a recipe calls for a single sprig, the rest of the bunch can easily go to waste. Luckily, as long as the herbs are cooked, you can substitute long-lasting dried herbs; this works especially well with sage, rosemary, and thyme. Just use one-third the amount called for. You can also dry your own fresh herbs to keep them from going bad.

- When **flank steak** is tempting you for a stir-fry or a spice-rubbed main, all you'll need is **1 pound**.

- Scallops can vary in size and weight, and, as with most seafood, you don't want to buy too much because it is very perishable. Ask your seafood monger for **12 ounces of large sea scallops,** which is the perfect amount for two.

- Stuck at the seafood counter guessing how much shrimp you need? For most recipes where the shrimp takes center stage, you'll need about **12 ounces of shell-on shrimp**.

- For a comforting dish of steamed **mussels**, pick up **2 pounds**. (They are usually packaged in convenient two-pound net bags.)

handy equipment for two

Cooking for two often calls for the inventive use of standard kitchen basics, such as a loaf pan that can be used to make the perfect size lasagna. But sometimes for-two recipes simply require a smaller version of everyday essentials, such as an 8-inch skillet for frittatas or a small saucepan for polenta or couscous. Fortunately, these items are inexpensive and widely available in stores and online. Here's a list of some of the equipment we reach for when scaling recipes down to size.

sheet pans, large and small
Rimmed baking sheets, also called half-sheet pans, get lots of use in the test kitchen; we use them every day for tasks such as roasting oven fries or root vegetables. Slipping a wire cooling rack inside (to elevate food for increased air circulation) makes these pans even more versatile—it's our go-to setup for roasting and broiling meats. Our favorite rimmed baking sheet (the **Nordic Ware Baker's Half Sheet**) measures 16½ by 11½ inches; since you won't always need such a large sheet pan when cooking for two, we recommend buying some smaller sheet pans (known as quarter-sheet pans) for small-scale recipes that don't require quite as much baking surface. Smaller sheet pans are also easier to store and clean.

small, medium, and large saucepans
When cooking for two, we frequently reach for a saucepan instead of a larger pot such as a Dutch oven. For instance, we use a large saucepan for our Clams with Israeli Couscous, Kielbasa, and Fennel. To make Weeknight Beef Stew, a medium saucepan is just right. And small saucepans are perfect for melting just a little butter or making a batch of rice for two. We recommend you have at least one saucepan in each size. Our winning small nonstick saucepan is the **Calphalon Contemporary Nonstick 2½ Quart Shallow Saucepan with Cover** and our favorite large saucepan is the **All-Clad Stainless 4-Qt Sauce Pan**.

cast iron skillets
Few pieces of kitchen gear improve after years of heavy use, but this is absolutely true of cast-iron skillets. As you cook in a cast-iron pan, it gradually takes on a natural, slick patina that releases food easily. Cast-iron pans are virtually indestructible and easily restored if mistreated. Their special talent is heat retention, making them ideal for browning and shallow frying. Though our favorite cast-iron pans (**Lodge Classic Cast Iron Skillet, 12"** and **Le Creuset Signature 11¾" Iron Handle Skillet**) are on the larger side, smaller ones are available; a 10-inch cast-iron skillet is a great size, particularly when you want a good sear but don't need a full 12-inch surface area.

traditional and nonstick skillets
Although a 12-inch skillet (both traditional and nonstick) is the size we use most often, once we started scaling down recipes to serve two we found that many required a smaller skillet—try to make just enough pan sauce for two steaks in a 12-inch skillet and it will overreduce and burn. We recommend investing in both a 10-inch and an 8-inch skillet. Note, however, that some of our for-two recipes—such as Skillet Pork Lo Mein—still require the surface area of a 12-inch pan, so for these recipes we recommend the **All-Clad d3 Stainless Steel 12" Fry Pan with Lid** or the **OXO Good Grips Non-Stick 12-inch Open Frypan**.

loaf pans
Almost everyone has a couple of loaf pans in their kitchen, which is a good thing because they come in handy when cooking for two—a loaf pan is the perfect alternative to a large baking dish when assembling a scaled-down casserole such as our Baked Manicotti. We take advantage of these smaller pans in other creative ways as well, using them to make sides such as Hands-Off Baked Brown Rice. Our preferred loaf pan (the **Williams Sonoma Goldtouch Nonstick Loaf Pan**) measures 8½ by 4½ inches.

small food processor
Owning a good food processor is like having a little motorized sous chef living in your cabinet. While we consider ours indispensable, standard food processors tend to be pricey and take up a lot of counter space. Though smaller processors can't do everything their full-size counterparts can, they are a helpful tool for budget- or space-conscious cooks. We use our **Cuisinart Elite Collection 4-Cup Chopper/Grinder** to make quick work of mincing, dicing, or grinding smaller quantities of ingredients; it is the perfect machine to chop a 10-ounce salmon fillet to make salmon cakes for two.

handheld mixer
While stand mixers are useful for heavy-duty tasks, a good handheld mixer is a practical (and cheaper) alternative if you don't have a ton of kitchen space or you simply want to avoid lugging out a big, heavy piece of equipment every time you need to whip egg yolks. Our favorite is the **KitchenAid 5-Speed Ultra Power Hand Mixer**.

lots of ramekins
Ramekins of various sizes are handy for making scaled-down desserts or individually portioned casseroles. Though our winning ramekins, **Le Creuset Stackable Ramekins**, hold 7½ ounces, other sizes are available and are useful to have on hand. (For example, we discovered that 12-ounce ramekins were the perfect size for individual Chicken Pot Pies.)

small baking dishes
Small baking dishes are the perfect vessel for smaller gratins. For instance, we use an 8½ by 5½-inch baking dish for our Cauliflower Gratin. Look for gratin dishes with straight sides no higher than 2 inches; taller sides inhibit browning. Our favorite mini gratin dish is the 6-ounce **Le Creuset Heritage Petite Au Gratin Dish**.

dinners for two, for any occasion

This collection encompasses a wide variety of appealing, modern dinners scaled down for two. No matter the occasion—whether you're celebrating an anniversary at home with a nice meal, or you're in a time crunch and have only 45 minutes to cook dinner on a busy weeknight—we've covered it all. Many recipes are complete dinners (such as Spice-Rubbed Flank Steak with Spicy Corn and Black Bean Salad or Almond-Crusted Chicken Breasts with Wilted Spinach-Orange Salad), while others are essential mains you'll want to round out with a suggested side or two (see pages 164–169). Our goal was to make meal planning as fun, easy, and fuss-free as possible to ensure you get the most out of this book.

date night in
Honey-Roasted Cornish Game Hens + Quinoa Pilaf

Herb-Crusted Beef Tenderloin + Mashed Potatoes

Steak au Poivre with Brandied Cream Sauce + Roasted Sweet Potatoes

Herb-Rubbed Pork Tenderloin with Fennel and Artichokes

Potato Gnocchi with Brown Butter–Sage Sauce + Basic Green Salad

italian bistro at home
Chicken Parmesan

Spaghetti and Turkey-Pesto Meatballs

Baked Manicotti + Basic Green Salad

no need for takeout
Sichuan Orange Chicken with Broccoli + Simple White Rice

Teriyaki-Glazed Steak Tips + Classic Rice Pilaf

Singapore Noodles with Shrimp

meatless meals
Asparagus and Goat Cheese Frittata + Basic Green Salad

Garlicky Spaghetti with Lemon and Pine Nuts + Roasted Broccoli

Soba Noodles with Roasted Eggplant and Sesame

Stuffed Acorn Squash with Barley

game day grub
Juicy Pub-Style Burgers + Sweet and Tangy Coleslaw

Spice-Rubbed Flank Steak with Spicy Corn and Black Bean Salad

Crispy Salmon Cakes with Sweet and Tangy Tartar Sauce + Sweet and Tangy Coleslaw

Easy Skillet Cheese Pizza + Basic Green Salad

going global
Chicken and Chorizo Paella

Miso-Marinated Salmon + Simple White Rice

Pad Thai

45 minutes or less
Pan-Roasted Filets Mignons with Asparagus and Garlic-Herb Butter

Orecchiette with Broccoli Rabe and Italian Sausage

Pasta with Beans, Chard, and Rosemary

list of recipes

chicken pot pie

why this recipe works Chicken pot pie is an indulgent cold-weather dinner, but when cooking for only two, a whole pot pie is overwhelming—not to mention a lot of work to feed a small household. We wanted a recipe that was streamlined enough to make a small batch worthwhile. Two 12-ounce ramekins had enough depth to accommodate plenty of filling and enough surface area to allow for a good amount of crust. For the chicken, we found that one 8-ounce boneless, skinless breast was just right. We whipped up a traditional white sauce enhanced with thyme and parsley, plus a dash of soy sauce to punch up the flavor. With the sauce assembled, we added the chicken breast and simmered everything briefly. Once the chicken was cooked, we shredded it before returning it to the sauce; this ensured tender pieces of chicken in every bite. For the vegetables, we went with peas and carrots. The peas we could simply stir into the sauce right before baking the pies. The carrots, however, required more time to soften, so we jump-started their cooking by sautéing them with onion and celery. For ease, we used store-bought crust, first baking the dough rounds on their own on a baking sheet and then letting them finish baking atop the pies. We use ovensafe 12-ounce ramekins to make these pot pies, but if you don't own any, you can use 14-ounce disposable mini loaf pans; cut the crust to fit.

serves 2
total time: 1 hour 30 minutes

1 package store-bought pie dough

2 tablespoons unsalted butter

2 carrots, peeled and sliced ¼ inch thick

1 small onion, chopped fine

1 small celery rib, sliced ¼ inch thick

Salt and pepper

2 garlic cloves, minced

1 teaspoon minced fresh thyme

3 tablespoons all-purpose flour

1¾ cups chicken broth

⅓ cup heavy cream

½ teaspoon soy sauce

1 (8-ounce) boneless, skinless chicken breast, trimmed

¼ cup frozen peas

2 teaspoons minced fresh parsley

¼ teaspoon lemon juice

1. Adjust oven rack to middle position and heat oven to 450 degrees. Line rimmed baking sheet with parchment paper. Unroll dough onto prepared sheet. Using 12-ounce ovensafe ramekin as guide, cut out 2 rounds of dough about ½ inch larger than mouth of ramekin. Fold excess dough under and crimp outer ½ inch of dough, then cut 3 vents in center of each dough round. Bake until crusts just begin to brown and no longer look raw, about 7 minutes; set aside.

2. Meanwhile, melt butter in medium saucepan over medium heat. Add carrots, onion, celery, and ½ teaspoon salt and cook until vegetables are softened and browned, 8 to 10 minutes. Stir in garlic and thyme and cook until fragrant, about 30 seconds. Stir in flour and cook for 1 minute.

3. Slowly whisk in broth, cream, and soy sauce, scraping up any browned bits. Nestle chicken into sauce and bring to simmer. Cover, reduce heat to medium-low, and cook until chicken registers 160 degrees, 10 to 15 minutes. Transfer chicken to plate; let cool slightly. Using 2 forks, shred chicken into bite-size pieces.

4. Meanwhile, return saucepan to medium heat and simmer sauce until thickened and reduced to 2 cups, about 5 minutes. Off heat, return shredded chicken and any accumulated juices to saucepan. Stir in peas, parsley, and lemon juice and season with salt and pepper to taste.

5. Divide filling between two 12-ounce ovensafe ramekins and place parbaked crusts on top of filling. Place pot pies on baking sheet and bake until crusts are deep golden brown and filling is bubbling, 10 to 15 minutes. Let pot pies cool for 10 minutes before serving.

chicken parmesan

why this recipe works Chicken Parmesan is a perennial favorite, but its multiple components turn it into a time-consuming affair. We wanted to simplify this dish to make it feasible for two. Tasters liked the fresh, bright tomato flavor of canned whole tomatoes, so we pulsed them in a food processor to a pleasantly coarse texture. Garlic sautéed in olive oil provided a rich backbone, and basil, sugar, and salt rounded out our sauce. We pounded our chicken breasts to ensure an even thickness (and thus, even cooking), and then we coated them in flour, dipped them in egg, and rolled them in a coating of panko bread crumbs and Parmesan. Pan-frying the chicken produced a well-browned crust that stayed crispy even when topped with melted cheese. Spooning the sauce over the cheese, not the chicken, also ensured a crispy crust. We saved the remaining sauce for tossing with a classic side of spaghetti.

serves 2
total time: 1 hour

sauce
1 (28-ounce) can whole peeled tomatoes, drained

2 tablespoons extra-virgin olive oil

2 garlic cloves, minced

2 tablespoons chopped fresh basil

¼ teaspoon sugar, plus extra as needed

Salt

chicken and spaghetti
¼ cup all-purpose flour

1 large egg

¾ cup panko bread crumbs

¼ cup grated Parmesan cheese

2 (6- to 8-ounce) boneless, skinless chicken breasts, trimmed and pounded to ½-inch thickness

Salt and pepper

6 tablespoons vegetable oil

1 ounce whole-milk mozzarella cheese, shredded (¼ cup)

1 ounce fontina cheese, shredded (¼ cup)

1 tablespoon chopped fresh basil

4 ounces spaghetti

1. for the sauce Pulse tomatoes in food processor until coarsely ground, 6 to 8 pulses. Cook oil and garlic in medium saucepan over medium heat, stirring often, until garlic is fragrant but not browned, about 2 minutes. Stir in tomatoes, bring to simmer, and cook until sauce is slightly thickened, 10 to 15 minutes. Off heat, stir in basil and sugar and season with salt and extra sugar to taste; cover to keep warm.

2. for the chicken and spaghetti Adjust oven rack 4 inches from broiler element and heat broiler. Spread flour in shallow dish. Beat egg in second shallow dish. Combine panko and Parmesan in third shallow dish. Pat chicken dry with paper towels and season with salt and pepper. Working with 1 breast at a time, dredge breasts in flour, dip in egg, then coat with panko mixture, pressing gently to adhere.

3. Line large plate with triple layer of paper towels. Heat oil in 10-inch nonstick skillet over medium-high heat until shimmering. Place chicken in skillet and cook until golden brown on both sides, 4 to 6 minutes per side. Drain chicken on paper towel–lined plate, then transfer to rimmed baking sheet. Combine mozzarella and fontina in bowl. Sprinkle cheese mixture evenly over chicken, covering as much surface area as possible. Broil until cheese is melted and beginning to brown, 2 to 4 minutes. Transfer chicken to serving platter, top each breast with 2 tablespoons tomato sauce, and sprinkle with basil.

4. Meanwhile, bring 4 quarts water to boil in large pot. Add pasta and 1 tablespoon salt and cook, stirring often, until al dente. Reserve ½ cup cooking water, then drain pasta and return it to pot. Add remaining sauce and toss to combine. Adjust consistency with reserved cooking water as needed and season with salt and pepper to taste. Serve chicken with pasta.

almond-crusted chicken breasts with wilted spinach–orange salad

why this recipe works When leafy greens are paired with sautéed chicken, a simple salad becomes a satisfying, one-dish meal. We wanted to create an easy recipe for such a dish, and thought adding nuts to the coating of the chicken would make for a heartier, more elegant meal. We started by pounding two boneless, skinless chicken breasts to the same thickness to ensure that they would cook evenly. A combination of ground almonds and panko created a rich-tasting crust that was both light and crisp. After dipping the chicken breasts in beaten egg and then the nut-panko mixture, we let them sit for a few minutes to help the coating adhere before pan-frying. To save time and dishes, we created a warm dressing right in the same skillet we had used to cook the chicken. Pieces of juicy orange provided a nice contrast to the rich nut crust of the chicken, and lightly browning them enhanced their sweetness. A little shallot and orange zest provided another layer of flavor. We used the hot dressing to wilt the spinach that served as the base of our warm, substantial salad. It should take about 15 to 20 seconds to process the almonds into fine crumbs—don't overprocess or the nuts will become oily.

serves 2
total time: 30 minutes

1 large egg

½ teaspoon Dijon mustard

2 oranges (1 orange grated to yield ¾ teaspoon zest and then cut into 4 wedges for serving, 1 orange peeled, pith removed, quartered through ends, and sliced crosswise into ¼-inch-thick pieces)

Salt and pepper

½ cup sliced almonds, processed to fine crumbs in food processor

¼ cup panko bread crumbs

2 (6- to 8-ounce) boneless, skinless chicken breasts, trimmed and pounded to ½-inch thickness

¼ cup vegetable oil

2½ ounces (2½ cups) baby spinach

1 small shallot, minced

1. Adjust oven rack to middle position and heat oven to 200 degrees. Lightly beat egg, mustard, ½ teaspoon zest, ¼ teaspoon salt, and ⅛ teaspoon pepper in shallow dish. Combine almonds and panko in separate shallow dish. Pat chicken dry with paper towels. Working with 1 breast at a time, dip breasts into egg mixture using tongs, turning to coat well and allowing excess to drip off, then coat with nut mixture, pressing gently to adhere. Transfer breaded chicken to wire rack set in rimmed baking sheet.

2. Heat 3 tablespoons oil in 10-inch nonstick skillet over medium-high heat until just smoking. Cook chicken until golden brown and crisp on first side, about 2½ minutes. Using tongs, flip chicken; reduce heat to medium and continue to cook until second side is deep golden brown and crisp, about 2 minutes longer. Transfer chicken to paper towel–lined plate and place plate in oven. Discard oil in skillet and wipe skillet clean with paper towels.

3. Place spinach in a large bowl. Heat remaining 1 tablespoon oil in now-empty skillet over medium heat until just smoking. Add orange pieces and cook until lightly browned around edges, 1 to 1½ minutes. Remove pan from heat and add shallot, remaining ¼ teaspoon zest, ⅛ teaspoon salt, and pinch pepper and allow residual heat to soften shallot, about 30 seconds. Pour warm dressing with oranges over spinach and toss gently to wilt. Remove chicken from oven and serve immediately with salad and orange wedges.

chicken saltimbocca

why this recipe works This classic Italian dish features tender chicken breasts topped with crispy prosciutto and earthy sage and finished with a bright, elegant pan sauce. But many versions take the dish too far from its simple roots, with loads of breading, cheese, and other extras that overwhelm the main ingredients. We wanted to keep the focus on the chicken, prosciutto, and sage and make this dish simple enough for a weeknight dinner for two. We started with chicken cutlets, which we floured to ensure even browning. Using thinly sliced prosciutto prevented its flavor from overwhelming the dish. A single fried sage leaf is the usual garnish, but for even more sage flavor, we sprinkled minced fresh sage over the floured chicken before adding the prosciutto. Since all four cutlets fit in the skillet at once, this dish was quick to cook, leaving us time to stir together an easy pan sauce to tie the dish together. If you can't find chicken cutlets, buy two boneless, skinless chicken breasts and slice your own. Do not buy shaved prosciutto. The prosciutto slices should be large enough to fully cover one side of each cutlet; if the slices are too large, simply cut them down to size.

serves 2
total time: 30 minutes

¼ cup plus ½ teaspoon all-purpose flour

4 (4-ounce) chicken cutlets, ¼ inch thick, trimmed

Salt and pepper

2 teaspoons minced fresh sage, plus 4 large fresh leaves

4 thin slices prosciutto (2 ounces)

2 tablespoons extra-virgin olive oil, plus extra as needed

1 small shallot, minced

⅓ cup chicken broth

¼ cup dry vermouth or dry white wine

1 tablespoon unsalted butter, chilled

2 teaspoons minced fresh parsley

1 teaspoon lemon juice

1. Spread ¼ cup flour in shallow dish. Pat chicken dry with paper towels and season with pepper. Working with 1 cutlet at a time, dredge cutlets in flour. Sprinkle 1 side of each cutlet with minced sage, then top with 1 slice prosciutto and press firmly to help it adhere.

2. Heat oil in 12-inch skillet over medium-high heat until shimmering. Add sage leaves and cook until leaves begin to change color and are fragrant, 15 to 20 seconds. Using slotted spoon, transfer sage leaves to paper towel–lined plate.

3. Place cutlets, prosciutto side down, in oil left in skillet and cook over medium-high heat until golden brown on first side, about 2 minutes. Flip cutlets and continue to cook until lightly browned on second side, about 1 minute longer; transfer to plate and tent with aluminum foil.

4. Pour off all but 1 teaspoon oil from skillet (or add more oil if necessary). Add shallot and cook over medium heat until softened, about 2 minutes. Stir in remaining ½ teaspoon flour and cook for 1 minute. Whisk in broth and vermouth, scraping up any browned bits. Bring to simmer and cook until sauce is slightly thickened and reduced to ⅓ cup, 3 to 5 minutes.

5. Return cutlets to skillet, prosciutto side up, along with any accumulated juices, and simmer until heated through, about 30 seconds; transfer cutlets to serving platter.

6. Off heat, whisk butter, parsley, and lemon juice into sauce and season with salt and pepper to taste. Pour sauce over cutlets, garnish with fried sage leaves, and serve.

chicken piccata

why this recipe works Chicken piccata is a simple dish that should be easy to get right. But many recipes miss the mark with extraneous ingredients or paltry amounts of lemon juice and capers. We wanted properly cooked chicken and a streamlined sauce that would keep the star ingredients at the forefront. To ensure that the chicken cooked evenly, we used an easy approach to preparing and cooking chicken cutlets. First, we cut each chicken breast in half crosswise. Next we halved the thicker portion horizontally to make three similar-size pieces that required only minimal pounding to become cutlets. We salted the cutlets briefly to boost their ability to retain moisture and then lightly coated them in flour, which aided browning and protected the delicate cutlets. We seared the chicken quickly on both sides and set it aside while making the sauce. Including both lemon juice and lemon slices in the sauce added complexity and textural appeal. We then returned the cutlets to the pan to cook through and to release any excess starch from the flour into the sauce, eliminating a gummy coating. Plenty of briny capers and a few tablespoons of butter finished the sauce, while a sprinkling of parsley added a final burst of freshness. Serve with Simple White Rice (page 164), Mashed Potatoes (page 166), or a steamed vegetable.

serves 2
total time: 50 minutes

2 (6- to 8-ounce) boneless, skinless chicken breasts, trimmed

Kosher salt and pepper

1 large lemon

½ cup all-purpose flour

2 tablespoons plus 1 teaspoon vegetable oil

1 small shallot, minced

½ teaspoon minced garlic

½ cup chicken broth

1½ tablespoons unsalted butter, cut into 3 pieces

1 tablespoon capers, drained

1½ teaspoons minced fresh parsley

1. Cut each chicken breast in half crosswise, then cut thick half in half horizontally, creating 3 cutlets of similar thickness. Place cutlets between sheets of plastic wrap and gently pound to even ¼-inch thickness. Place cutlets in bowl and toss with 1 teaspoon salt and ¼ teaspoon pepper. Set aside for 15 minutes.

2. Meanwhile, halve lemon lengthwise. Trim ends from 1 half, halve lengthwise again, then slice crosswise ¼ inch thick; set aside. Juice remaining half and set aside 1½ tablespoons juice.

3. Spread flour in shallow dish. Working with 1 cutlet at a time, dredge cutlets in flour, shaking gently to remove excess. Place on wire rack set in rimmed baking sheet. Heat 2 tablespoons oil in 12-inch skillet over medium-high heat until just smoking. Place

cutlets in skillet, reduce heat to medium, and cook until golden brown on first side, 2 to 3 minutes. Flip and cook until golden brown on second side, 2 to 3 minutes. Return cutlets to wire rack.

4. Add remaining 1 teaspoon oil and shallot to skillet and cook until softened, 30 seconds. Add garlic and cook until fragrant, about 30 seconds. Add broth, reserved lemon juice, and reserved lemon slices and bring to simmer, scraping up any browned bits.

5. Add cutlets to sauce and simmer for 4 minutes, flipping halfway through simmering. Transfer cutlets to platter. Sauce should be thickened to consistency of heavy cream; if not, simmer 1 minute longer. Off heat, whisk in butter. Stir in capers and parsley. Season with salt and pepper to taste. Spoon sauce over chicken and serve.

parmesan and basil–stuffed chicken with roasted carrots

why this recipe works Stuffed chicken breasts may sound like a dish best reserved for entertaining, but they are actually quite doable as an easy meal for two. The key? A super simple stuffing. We started with a no-fuss cream cheese filling featuring basil, garlic, and a hefty ½ cup of savory Parmesan. Rather than attempt an overly complicated stuffing technique, we simply spooned the filling under the skin of bone-in chicken breasts; the skin held the filling in place, and the meat emerged from the oven moist and juicy. Brushing the skin with melted butter and baking the breasts in a 450-degree oven ensured crisp, golden-brown skin. We also wanted to serve a tasty vegetable alongside our chicken to complete the meal, so we tossed carrots with melted butter and a little brown sugar and roasted them with the chicken until perfectly softened and caramelized. Be sure to spread the carrots in an even layer halfway through roasting to ensure that they cook through and brown properly. It is important to buy chicken breasts with the skin still attached and intact; otherwise, the stuffing will leak out. If using kosher chicken, do not brine. If brining the chicken, do not season with salt in step 2.

serves 2
total time: 1 hour

1 ounce Parmesan cheese, grated (½ cup)

1 ounce cream cheese, softened

2 tablespoons chopped fresh basil

1 tablespoon extra-virgin olive oil

1 small garlic clove, minced

Salt and pepper

2 (12-ounce) bone-in split chicken breasts, trimmed and brined if desired (see page 169)

1 tablespoon unsalted butter, melted

6 small carrots, peeled and sliced ½ inch thick on bias

1½ teaspoons packed dark brown sugar

1. Adjust oven rack to middle position and heat oven to 450 degrees. Line rimmed baking sheet with aluminum foil. Mix Parmesan, cream cheese, basil, oil, garlic, pinch salt, and pinch pepper together in bowl.

2. Pat chicken dry with paper towels and season with salt and pepper. Use your fingers to gently loosen center portion of skin covering each breast. Using spoon, place half of cheese mixture underneath skin over center of each breast. Gently press on skin to spread out cheese mixture.

3. Arrange chicken, skin side up, on half of baking sheet. Brush chicken with half of melted butter. Toss carrots with remaining melted butter and sugar and season with salt and pepper. Mound carrots in pile on baking sheet, opposite chicken.

4. Bake until chicken registers 160 degrees and carrots are browned and tender, 30 to 35 minutes, rotating sheet and spreading out carrots into even layer halfway through baking. Let chicken and carrots rest on sheet for 5 minutes before serving.

pan-roasted chicken breasts with garlic and sherry sauce

why this recipe works Pan-roasting bone-in chicken breasts yields tender meat and crisp skin; it also leaves plenty of flavorful browned bits in the skillet to serve as the foundation for a flavorful sauce. The result is an easy, elegant dinner for two people. We started by brining the chicken to help the delicate breast meat stay moist and flavorful. To encourage crisp skin, we patted the brined meat dry with paper towels to ensure that the skin would sear rather than steam. We browned the chicken on both sides on the stovetop before moving the skillet to the oven. Cooking the chicken at 450 degrees allowed the skin to crisp while the meat cooked through relatively quickly. Finally, while the chicken rested, we built a savory pan sauce with kitchen staples like garlic, sherry, and chicken broth. If using kosher chicken, do not brine. If brining the chicken, do not season with salt in step 1.

serves 2
total time: 1 hour

2 (12-ounce) bone-in split chicken breasts, trimmed and brined if desired (see page 169)

Salt and pepper

2 teaspoons vegetable oil

3 garlic cloves, sliced thin

½ teaspoon all-purpose flour

½ cup chicken broth

¼ cup dry sherry

2 sprigs fresh thyme

1 tablespoon butter, chilled

½ teaspoon lemon juice

1. Adjust oven rack to lowest position and heat oven to 450 degrees. Pat chicken dry with paper towels and season with salt and pepper.

2. Heat oil in 10-inch ovensafe skillet over medium-high heat until just smoking. Lay chicken skin side down in skillet and cook until well browned on first side, 6 to 8 minutes, reducing heat if pan begins to scorch. Flip chicken and continue to cook until lightly browned, about 3 minutes.

3. Flip chicken skin side down and transfer skillet to oven. Roast until chicken registers 160 degrees, 15 to 18 minutes.

4. Using potholders (skillet handle will be hot), remove skillet from oven. Transfer chicken to serving platter and tent loosely with aluminum foil.

5. Being careful of hot skillet handle, pour off all but 1 tablespoon fat from skillet, add garlic, and cook over medium heat until softened, about 2 minutes. Stir in flour and cook for 1 minute. Whisk in broth, sherry, and thyme sprigs, scraping up any browned bits. Bring to simmer and cook until slightly thickened, about 5 minutes. Stir in any accumulated chicken juices and simmer for 30 seconds. Off heat, remove thyme sprigs and whisk in butter and lemon juice. Season with salt and pepper to taste. Pour sauce over chicken and serve.

variation

pan-roasted chicken breasts with pomegranate and balsamic sauce Reduce amount of chicken broth to ¼ cup. Substitute 1 minced small shallot for garlic, ½ cup pomegranate juice for sherry, and ½ teaspoon balsamic vinegar for lemon juice.

honey-roasted cornish game hens

why this recipe works Cornish game hens are perfect for elegant dinners for two: Each diner gets a whole bird, making for a beautiful presentation and, ideally, offering all the benefits of a whole chicken (a combination of light and dark meat, crisp skin) without all the leftovers. Plus, they're inexpensive and quick-cooking. But these small birds also suffer from many of the same pitfalls as whole chickens: The white and dark meat cook at different rates, and it can be a challenge to crisp the skin before the meat dries out. We roasted our birds on a wire rack set in a baking sheet to allow the heat to circulate around them. Turning the birds once partway through cooking helped the meat cook more evenly. We also significantly increased the oven temperature toward the end of roasting to give the skin rich color without drying out the meat. A glaze of honey and cider vinegar gave the birds great flavor and glossy exteriors. If using kosher hens, do not brine. If brining the hens, omit the salt in step 1.

serves 2
total time: 1 hour 20 minutes

Salt and pepper

½ teaspoon paprika

2 (1¼- to 1½-pound) whole Cornish game hens, giblets discarded, brined if desired (see page 169)

5 tablespoons honey

5 teaspoons cider vinegar

2 teaspoons plus ½ cup water

1 teaspoon cornstarch

½ cup chicken broth

½ teaspoon minced fresh thyme

1 tablespoon unsalted butter, chilled

1. Adjust oven rack to middle position and heat oven to 400 degrees. Set wire rack in rimmed baking sheet. Combine ¾ teaspoon salt, paprika, and ¼ teaspoon pepper in bowl.

2. Pat hens dry with paper towels. Sprinkle all over with salt mixture and rub in mixture with your hands to coat evenly. Tuck wingtips behind backs and lay hens breast side down on prepared rack. Roast hens until backs are golden brown, about 25 minutes.

3. Meanwhile, bring ¼ cup honey and 1 tablespoon vinegar to simmer in small saucepan over medium-high heat. Whisk 2 teaspoons water and ½ teaspoon cornstarch together in small bowl, then whisk into saucepan. Continue to simmer glaze until thickened, 1 to 2 minutes. Remove from heat and cover to keep warm.

4. Remove hens from oven and brush backs with one-third of glaze. Flip hens breast side up and brush with half of remaining glaze. Continue to roast for 15 minutes.

5. Remove hens from oven and increase oven temperature to 450 degrees. Pour remaining ½ cup water and broth into baking sheet. Brush hens with remaining glaze and continue to roast until glaze is spotty brown and breasts register 160 degrees and thighs register 175 degrees, 5 to 10 minutes longer. Transfer hens to serving platter and let rest, uncovered, for 10 minutes.

6. Pour liquid from sheet into now-empty saucepan and let settle for 5 minutes. Using large spoon, skim excess fat from surface of liquid. Stir in thyme and remaining 1 tablespoon honey, bring to simmer, and cook until sauce is reduced to ½ cup, 2 to 6 minutes.

7. Whisk remaining 2 teaspoons vinegar and remaining ½ teaspoon cornstarch together in bowl, then whisk into saucepan. Continue to simmer sauce until thickened, 1 to 2 minutes. Stir in any accumulated juices; simmer for 30 seconds. Off heat, whisk in butter and season with salt and pepper to taste. Serve hens with sauce.

moroccan chicken with green olives

why this recipe works Traditional North African tagines—aromatic braises of meat, vegetables, and fruits—are labor-intensive and call for hard-to-find ingredients. We came up with a few timesaving tricks to make a tagine for two featuring chicken, lemon, and olives. First, we swapped out bone-in chicken thighs for quicker-cooking boneless thighs. Poaching the chicken in a flavorful broth infused it with flavor and ensured that the chicken was tender. Instead of calling for a laundry list of spices, we used garam masala, an Indian spice mix, and gave it a flavor boost with paprika. Coarsely chopped dried figs added a hint of sweetness, while green olives provided some brininess. A sprinkle of cilantro and splash of lemon juice brightened the sauce. Look for large, pitted green olives at the olive bar in the supermarket. Pimento-stuffed olives can be substituted for the large green olives in a pinch. Serve with couscous or Simple White Rice (page 164).

serves 2
total time: 45 minutes

1 tablespoon extra-virgin olive oil

1 small onion, halved and sliced thin

1 (3-inch) strip lemon zest plus 1½ teaspoons juice

2 garlic cloves, minced

1 teaspoon garam masala

½ teaspoon paprika

½ cup chicken broth

¼ cup pitted large green olives, chopped coarse

¼ cup dried figs, stemmed and chopped coarse

4 (3-ounce) boneless, skinless chicken thighs, trimmed

Salt and pepper

1 tablespoon minced fresh cilantro

1. Heat oil in 10-inch skillet over medium heat until shimmering. Add onion and cook until softened, about 5 minutes. Stir in lemon zest, garlic, garam masala, and paprika and cook until fragrant, about 30 seconds. Stir in broth, olives, and figs, scraping up any browned bits.

2. Season chicken with salt and pepper, lay in skillet, and bring to simmer. Reduce heat to medium-low, cover, and simmer until chicken is very tender, about 15 minutes; transfer chicken to serving platter and tent loosely with aluminum foil.

3. Discard lemon zest. Continue to simmer sauce until slightly thickened, about 3 minutes. Stir in any accumulated chicken juices and simmer for 30 seconds. Stir in cilantro and lemon juice and season with salt and pepper to taste. Pour sauce over chicken and serve.

three-cup chicken

serves 2
total time: 50 minutes

why this recipe works Originating in Dadu (modern Beijing), Three-Cup Chicken, or *San Bei Ji*, was named for its sparse ingredient list: a sauce made with 1 cup each of soy sauce, sesame oil, and rice wine. Eventually adopted by neighboring Taiwan, it has evolved into a national dish of sorts. We aimed to scale this dish to serve two, and while we wanted to remain true to its roots, we hoped to incorporate some additional flavors and ingredients for a dish with a bit more depth and complexity. First, we streamlined prep by calling for boneless, skinless chicken thighs, which eliminated the need to butcher a whole chicken. For deep flavor, we marinated the chicken in the requisite soy sauce and rice wine along with a bit of brown sugar. Thinly sliced scallions, ginger, garlic cloves, and red pepper flakes contributed a balance of flavors and textures. Eliminating the step of browning allowed the chicken and sauce to cook in about 30 minutes, making this recipe a viable weeknight dinner option. A bit of cornstarch mixed with water thickened the sauce to a perfect consistency. Thai basil added welcome freshness, and toasted sesame oil stirred in at the end provided a final flavor punch. We prefer the flavor of Thai basil in this recipe, but Italian basil can be substituted. For a spicier dish, use the larger amount of red pepper flakes. Serve with Simple White Rice (page 164).

3 tablespoons soy sauce

3 tablespoons Chinese rice wine or dry sherry

1½ teaspoons packed brown sugar

12 ounces boneless, skinless chicken thighs, trimmed and cut into 2-inch pieces

1½ tablespoons vegetable oil

1 (1-inch) piece ginger, peeled, halved lengthwise, and sliced thin into half rounds

6 garlic cloves, peeled and halved lengthwise

¼–½ teaspoon red pepper flakes

3 scallions, white and green parts separated and sliced thin on bias

½ teaspoon cornstarch mixed with 1½ teaspoons water

1½ teaspoons toasted sesame oil

½ cup Thai basil leaves, large leaves sliced in half lengthwise

1. Whisk together soy sauce, rice wine, and sugar in medium bowl. Add chicken, toss to coat, and set aside.

2. Heat vegetable oil, ginger, garlic, and pepper flakes in 10-inch nonstick skillet over medium-low heat. Cook, stirring frequently, until garlic is golden brown and beginning to soften, 8 to 10 minutes.

3. Add chicken and marinade to skillet, increase heat to medium-high, and bring to simmer. Reduce heat to medium-low and simmer, stirring occasionally, for 10 minutes. Stir in scallion whites and continue to cook until chicken is tender, 8 to 10 minutes longer.

4. Re-whisk cornstarch mixture, then whisk into sauce; simmer until slightly thickened, about 1 minute. Remove skillet from heat and stir in sesame oil, scallion greens, and basil. Transfer to platter and serve.

sichuan orange chicken with broccoli

why this recipe works Sweet and spicy orange chicken is a takeout favorite; but while ordering in can be especially tempting on busy weeknights, in a household of two the inevitable leftovers are apt to go to waste. We wanted to create an easy version at home that would boast real orange flavor and make just enough for one two-person meal. A high-impact marinade consisting of orange juice, orange zest, sweet hoisin sauce, salty soy sauce, and spicy chili-garlic sauce thoroughly infused the chicken with flavor in only 10 minutes. The addition of broccoli made for a more substantial dish. Red bell pepper and scallion provided another layer of flavor, as well as color and textural contrast; steaming the vegetables in the skillet ensured a perfect crisp-tender texture. A smoking-hot skillet allowed the chicken to brown and cook through quickly without drying out. To make the chicken easier to slice, freeze it for 15 minutes. For a spicier dish, use the larger amount of chili-garlic sauce. Serve with Simple White Rice (page 164).

serves 2
total time: 45 minutes

2 tablespoons hoisin sauce

1 tablespoon soy sauce

2–3 teaspoons Asian chili-garlic sauce

2 teaspoons cornstarch

1 teaspoon grated orange zest plus ¼ cup juice

12 ounces boneless, skinless chicken breasts, trimmed and sliced ¼ inch thick

2 teaspoons toasted sesame oil

2 garlic cloves, minced

2 teaspoons grated fresh ginger

8 ounces broccoli florets, cut into 1-inch pieces

1 small red bell pepper, stemmed, seeded, and cut into 2-inch-long matchsticks

¼ cup water

1 scallion, sliced thin

1. Whisk hoisin, soy sauce, chili-garlic sauce, cornstarch, and orange zest and juice together in small bowl. Measure 1 tablespoon sauce into medium bowl, then stir in chicken and 1 teaspoon oil. Cover and marinate chicken in refrigerator for at least 10 minutes or up to 30 minutes. Meanwhile, in separate bowl, combine garlic, ginger, and remaining 1 teaspoon oil.

2. Cook broccoli, bell pepper, and water, covered, in 12-inch nonstick skillet over high heat until water is boiling and vegetables begin to soften, about 3 minutes. Uncover and continue to cook until water has evaporated and vegetables are crisp-tender, about 2 minutes; transfer to bowl.

3. Add chicken to now-empty skillet set over high heat and cook, breaking up any clumps, until lightly browned on all sides, about 6 minutes. Push chicken to sides of skillet. Add garlic mixture to center and cook, mashing mixture into skillet, until fragrant, about 30 seconds. Stir garlic mixture into chicken.

4. Stir in cooked vegetable mixture. Whisk sauce to recombine, then add to skillet. Cook, stirring constantly, until sauce is thickened, about 1 minute. Transfer to serving platter, sprinkle with scallion, and serve.

thai chicken with basil

why this recipe works Capturing the flavors of this traditional Thai dish required not only the right ingredients but also learning a whole new way to stir-fry. Stir-frying at a low temperature (versus the usual high-heat method) allowed us to add aromatics and basil at the beginning of cooking so they infused the dish with more of their flavor. Grinding the chicken in a food processor gave us coarse-textured meat that retained moisture during cooking. A combination of fish sauce, oyster sauce, and white vinegar added rich but bright flavor. Stirring in more basil at the end provided a fresh finish and bold flavor. For a milder version of the dish, remove the seeds and ribs from the chiles. If fresh Thai chiles are unavailable, substitute two serranos or one medium jalapeño. Serve with Simple White Rice (page 164).

serves 2
total time: 40 minutes

1 cup fresh basil leaves

2 green or red Thai chiles, stemmed

1 garlic clove, peeled

2½ teaspoons fish sauce, plus extra for serving

1½ teaspoons oyster sauce

½ teaspoon sugar, plus extra for serving

½ teaspoon distilled white vinegar, plus extra for serving

1 (8-ounce) boneless, skinless chicken breast, trimmed and cut into 2-inch pieces

1 shallot, sliced thin

1 tablespoon vegetable oil

Red pepper flakes

1. Pulse ½ cup basil, Thai chiles, and garlic in food processor until finely chopped, 10 to 12 pulses, scraping down sides of bowl as needed. Transfer 1½ teaspoons of basil mixture to small bowl and stir in 1½ teaspoons fish sauce, oyster sauce, sugar, and vinegar. Transfer remaining basil mixture to 10-inch nonstick skillet.

2. Without washing food processor bowl, pulse chicken and remaining 1 teaspoon fish sauce in food processor until meat is coarsely chopped, 6 to 8 pulses; transfer to medium bowl and refrigerate for 15 minutes.

3. Stir shallot and oil into basil mixture in skillet. Cook over medium-low heat, stirring constantly, until garlic and shallot are golden brown, 5 to 8 minutes. (Mixture should start to sizzle after about 1½ minutes; if it doesn't, adjust heat accordingly.)

4. Stir in chopped chicken and cook over medium heat, breaking up chicken with wooden spoon, until only traces of pink remain, 2 to 4 minutes. Add reserved basil–fish sauce mixture and cook, stirring constantly, until chicken is no longer pink, about 1 minute. Stir in remaining ½ cup basil leaves and cook, stirring constantly, until basil is wilted, 30 to 60 seconds. Serve immediately, passing extra fish sauce, sugar, vinegar, and pepper flakes separately.

chicken soft tacos

why this recipe works We like the convenience of using boneless, skinless chicken breasts to make shredded chicken tacos, but the lean meat can easily become dry and rubbery. We wanted a cooking technique that would guarantee tender, shreddable meat infused with spicy flavor, and we wanted just enough to be enjoyed by two. We poached the chicken in a simple but flavorful combination of sweet orange juice and savory Worcestershire sauce enhanced with cilantro, smoky chipotle, and fragrant garlic. Once the chicken was tender, we set it aside to rest while we reduced the poaching liquid to make a sauce. We then stirred in fresh cilantro and a bit of piquant yellow mustard, which nicely balanced the sweetness of the juice. Tossed in the sauce, dolloped with spicy chipotle sour cream, and wrapped in warm tortillas, our chicken filling was incredibly moist and laced with just the right amount of spice, heat, and tang. To make this dish more or less spicy, adjust the amount of chipotle chiles. Serve with your favorite taco toppings.

serves 2
total time: 50 minutes

1 teaspoon vegetable oil

3 garlic cloves, minced

1 teaspoon minced canned chipotle chile in adobo sauce

½ cup minced fresh cilantro

½ cup orange juice

1 tablespoon Worcestershire sauce

2 (6- to 8-ounce) boneless, skinless chicken breasts, trimmed and pounded to even thickness if necessary

1 teaspoon yellow mustard

Salt and pepper

½ cup sour cream

6 (6-inch) corn tortillas, warmed

1. Heat oil in 10-inch nonstick skillet over medium heat until shimmering. Stir in garlic and ½ teaspoon chipotle and cook until fragrant, about 30 seconds. Stir in 5 tablespoons cilantro, orange juice, and Worcestershire. Lay chicken in skillet and bring to simmer over medium-low heat, 10 to 15 minutes.

2. When liquid is simmering, flip chicken, cover, and continue to cook until chicken registers 160 degrees, 10 to 15 minutes.

3. Transfer chicken to cutting board, let cool slightly, then shred into bite-size pieces using 2 forks. Meanwhile, continue to simmer poaching liquid over medium heat until slightly thickened and reduced to ⅓ cup, about 2 minutes. Off heat, stir in mustard, 2 tablespoons cilantro, and shredded chicken and let sit until heated through, about 2 minutes. Season with salt and pepper to taste.

4. Combine sour cream, remaining ½ teaspoon chipotle, and remaining 1 tablespoon cilantro in bowl. Season with salt and pepper to taste. Serve chicken with warm tortillas and sour cream sauce.

chicken and chorizo paella

why this recipe works Paella is a fragrant Spanish rice dish featuring an impressive variety of meat, seafood, and vegetables. While delicious, it's undeniably a labor of love, and most recipes make enough to feed a small army. We wanted to translate this classic into a streamlined weeknight version, perfectly tailored for two people, with all the flavor of the original. A combination of chorizo sausage and chicken was hearty enough that we decided we could forgo the seafood altogether. A rich sofrito of onion, garlic, and tomato gave our dish a deep flavor base, and bright peas and briny olives added color and dimension. Just a pinch of saffron was enough to give our paella authentic Spanish flavor. We like to use short-grain Valencia rice for this dish, but you can substitute Arborio rice if you cannot find Valencia. Do not substitute long-grain rice. Look for large, pitted green olives at the olive bar in the supermarket. Pimento-stuffed olives can be substituted for the large green olives in a pinch. To make the chicken easier to slice, freeze it for 15 minutes.

serves 2
total time: 50 minutes

1½ cups water

½ cup Valencia or Arborio rice

Salt and pepper

1 (8-ounce) boneless, skinless chicken breast, trimmed and sliced ¼ inch thick

4 teaspoons vegetable oil

4 ounces Spanish-style chorizo sausage, halved lengthwise and sliced ¼ inch thick

1 small onion, chopped fine

¾ cup canned diced tomatoes, drained with juice reserved

2 garlic cloves, minced

⅛ teaspoon saffron threads, crumbled

¼ cup pitted large green olives, quartered

¼ cup frozen peas

1. Combine 1 cup water, rice, and ⅛ teaspoon salt in bowl. Cover and microwave until rice is softened and most of liquid is absorbed, 6 to 8 minutes.

2. Meanwhile, pat chicken dry with paper towels and season with salt and pepper. Heat 2 teaspoons oil in 10-inch nonstick skillet over medium-high heat until just smoking. Add chorizo and cook until lightly browned, about 2 minutes. Using slotted spoon, transfer chorizo to plate. Add chicken to fat left in skillet, breaking up any clumps, and cook until lightly browned on all sides, about 4 minutes; transfer to plate with chorizo.

3. Heat remaining 2 teaspoons oil in now-empty skillet over medium heat until shimmering. Add onion and cook until softened, about 5 minutes. Stir in tomatoes and cook until beginning to soften and darken, 3 to 5 minutes. Stir in garlic and saffron and cook until fragrant, about 30 seconds. Stir in remaining ½ cup water and reserved tomato juice, scraping up any browned bits. Stir in par-cooked rice, breaking up any large clumps, and bring to simmer. Reduce heat to medium-low, cover, and simmer until rice is tender and liquid is absorbed, 8 to 12 minutes.

4. Stir in browned chorizo and chicken and any accumulated juices, olives, and peas and increase heat to medium-high. Cook, uncovered, until bottom layer of rice is golden and crisp, about 5 minutes, rotating skillet halfway through cooking to ensure even browning. Season with salt and pepper to taste, and serve.

white chicken chili

why this recipe works We set out to create a dish for two that would provide all the appeal of a southwestern chili without the heft of the beef
variety. The answer? A white chicken chili packed with the flavors of bright
tomatillos and earthy poblano chiles. To achieve the right consistency for
our chili, we used two thickeners: flour and pureed hominy. Cooking the
flour briefly with the aromatics and spices—poblano chiles, onion, garlic,
cumin, and coriander—created a mixture that not only thickened the chili
but also built deep flavor. Pureeing a portion of the hominy with some
chicken broth gave our chili a luxuriously thick texture. And stirring in
½ cup of store-bought tomatillo salsa—also known as salsa verde—was a
quick and easy way to brighten up our chili's flavor at the end of cooking.
Both white hominy and yellow hominy will work in this chili; however, we
prefer the deeper flavor of white hominy here. To make this dish spicier,
add the chile seeds. Be careful not to overcook the chicken in step 4 or it
will taste dry. Serve with your favorite chili garnishes.

serves 2
total time: 50 minutes

1 (15-ounce) can white or yellow hominy, rinsed

2 cups chicken broth

1 tablespoon vegetable oil

2 poblano chiles, stemmed, seeded, and chopped

1 small onion, chopped fine

2 garlic cloves, minced

1 teaspoon ground cumin

1 teaspoon ground coriander

1 tablespoon all-purpose flour

12 ounces boneless, skinless chicken breasts, trimmed

Salt and pepper

½ cup jarred tomatillo salsa (salsa verde)

2 tablespoons minced fresh cilantro

1. Process 1 cup hominy and ½ cup broth in blender until smooth, about 10 seconds.

2. Heat oil in medium saucepan over medium heat until shimmer-ing. Add poblanos, onion, garlic, cumin, and coriander. Cook, stir-ring often, until vegetables are softened and spices are fragrant, about 5 minutes. Stir in flour and cook for 1 minute.

3. Slowly whisk in remaining 1½ cups broth, scraping up any browned bits and smoothing out any lumps. Stir in pureed hominy mixture and remaining hominy.

4. Season chicken with salt and pepper, add to chili mixture, and bring to simmer. Cover, reduce heat to medium-low, and simmer until chicken registers 160 degrees, 10 to 15 minutes, flipping chicken halfway through cooking. Transfer chicken to cutting board and let cool slightly. Using 2 forks, shred chicken into bite-size pieces.

5. Return chili to simmer, stir in shredded chicken and tomatillo salsa, and cook until heated through, about 2 minutes. Stir in cilantro and season with salt and pepper to taste. Serve.

spaghetti and turkey-pesto meatballs

why this recipe works Spaghetti and meatballs usually serve a crowd, so we wanted to create a scaled-down version of this dinnertime favorite with just the right amount of pasta and meatballs; and while we were at it, we hoped to put our own unique spin on this classic dish. Starting with the meatballs, we opted for 8 ounces of ground turkey, which offers a great, lighter alternative to the traditional beef and pork—as long as you can find a way to infuse it with flavor and prevent dryness. Convenient store-bought basil pesto helped us on both fronts: It offered big garlic and herb flavors without any prep, contributed a bit of richness, and kept our meatballs moist. Panko bread crumbs helped bind the mixture, and grated Parmesan added nutty, savory depth. After browning the meatballs, we whipped up a quick, simple tomato sauce by simmering canned crushed tomatoes with garlic (for aromatic flavor and bite) and sugar (to balance the tomatoes' acidity). We then added the meatballs to the sauce and let them simmer until they were cooked through. While the meatballs simmered, we boiled our pasta; just 6 ounces of spaghetti yielded the perfect amount for two. Be sure to use ground turkey, not ground turkey breast (also labeled 99 percent fat free), in this recipe. You can make your own pesto or use your favorite store-bought option from the refrigerated section of the supermarket—refrigerated pestos have a fresher flavor than the jarred pestos sold in the grocery aisles.

serves 2
total time: 45 minutes

8 ounces ground turkey

⅓ cup panko bread crumbs

¼ cup prepared basil pesto

Salt and pepper

1 tablespoon extra-virgin olive oil

1 garlic clove, minced

1 (28-ounce) can crushed tomatoes

¼ teaspoon sugar, plus extra for seasoning

6 ounces spaghetti

1 tablespoon shredded fresh basil

Grated Parmesan cheese

1. Using your hands, gently mix turkey, panko, pesto, ¼ teaspoon salt, and ⅛ teaspoon pepper in bowl until uniform.

2. Roll mixture into eight 1-inch meatballs. Heat oil in 10-inch skillet over medium-high heat until just smoking. Brown meatballs well on all sides, about 8 minutes; transfer to paper towel–lined plate.

3. Add garlic to fat left in skillet and cook over medium heat until fragrant, about 30 seconds. Stir in tomatoes and sugar, scraping up any browned bits. Bring to simmer and cook until sauce is slightly thickened, 5 to 8 minutes.

4. Return meatballs to skillet and reduce heat to medium-low. Cover and simmer gently, turning meatballs occasionally, until meatballs are cooked through, about 5 minutes. Season sauce with salt, pepper, and extra sugar to taste.

5. Meanwhile, bring 4 quarts water to boil in large pot. Add pasta and 1 tablespoon salt and cook, stirring often, until al dente. Reserve ½ cup cooking water, then drain pasta and return it to pot.

6. Add several large spoonfuls of sauce to pasta and toss to combine. Adjust consistency with reserved cooking water as needed and season with salt and pepper to taste. Divide pasta between 2 bowls, top each bowl with remaining sauce and meatballs, and sprinkle with basil. Serve, passing Parmesan separately.

weeknight beef stew

why this recipe works Beef stew recipes typically call for a lengthy simmering time to turn a tough, inexpensive cut like chuck roast meltingly tender; we wanted a weeknight-friendly, richly flavored beef stew that would cook in a fraction of the time and provide just enough for two. Instead of the usual chuck-eye roast we chose steak tips, which don't require a long cooking time to become tender. To mimic the flavor of a slow-cooked stew, we seared the beef in two batches to develop more fond. After sautéing onion and carrot in the flavorful fat left in the pan, we stirred in garlic, tomato paste, and a small amount of anchovy for extra meaty flavor and savory depth. A splash of wine helped us scrape up the flavorful browned bits in the pan, and soy sauce provided extra umami depth before serving. Steak tips, also known as flap meat, are sold as whole steak, cubes, and strips; look for either whole steak tips or strips that are easy to cut into small pieces for this recipe.

serves 2
total time: 1 hour

12 ounces sirloin steak tips, trimmed and cut into ½-inch pieces

Salt and pepper

4 teaspoons vegetable oil

1 small onion, chopped fine

1 carrot, peeled and sliced ¼ inch thick

2 garlic cloves, minced

1 teaspoon tomato paste

½ anchovy fillet, rinsed and minced

½ teaspoon minced fresh thyme or ⅛ teaspoon dried

1 tablespoon all-purpose flour

3 tablespoons dry red wine

1½ cups beef broth

1 small Yukon Gold potato (6 ounces), peeled and cut into ½-inch pieces

¼ cup frozen peas

1 teaspoon soy sauce

1 tablespoon minced fresh parsley

1. Pat beef dry with paper towels and season with salt and pepper. Heat 2 teaspoons oil in medium saucepan over medium-high heat until just smoking. Brown half of beef on all sides, 5 to 7 minutes; transfer to bowl. Repeat with remaining 2 teaspoons oil and remaining beef; transfer to bowl.

2. Add onion and carrot to fat left in saucepan and cook over medium heat until softened, about 5 minutes. Stir in garlic, tomato paste, anchovy, and thyme and cook until fragrant, about 30 seconds. Stir in flour and cook for 1 minute.

3. Slowly whisk in wine, scraping up any browned bits and smoothing out any lumps. Stir in broth and potato and bring to simmer. Reduce heat to medium-low, cover, and simmer until vegetables are tender, 15 to 20 minutes.

4. Stir in browned beef and any accumulated juices, peas, and soy sauce and simmer until stew is heated through, about 2 minutes. Season with salt and pepper to taste, sprinkle with parsley, and serve.

beef stroganoff

why this recipe works In its simplest, most elegant form, beef stroganoff is a dish of sautéed beef, mushrooms, and onion in a creamy sauce that is typically served over egg noodles. For a scaled-down version of this warm, comforting favorite, we knew time management would be key, so we opted for tender, quick-cooking filet mignon. By cooking the meat first and then slicing it, we were able to not only build considerable fond in the pan (a boon for the sauce's flavor) but also better control the meat's temperature, thus preventing overcooking. Beef broth formed the backbone of our sauce, and we imbued it with flavor by adding a bit of Dijon mustard for pungency and a splash of soy sauce for a meaty, savory quality. Cooking the egg noodles right in the skillet as the sauce thickened saved time and meant that this meal for two could be prepared in a single pan. We achieved just the right amount of creaminess by stirring in a dollop of sour cream, freshened up with a few snips of chives, just before serving. Look for a steak that is 1½ to 2 inches thick. White wine or vermouth can be used in place of the brandy.

serves 2
total time: 50 minutes

---

8 ounces white mushrooms, trimmed and quartered

1 (8-ounce) center-cut filet mignon, trimmed and halved crosswise

Salt and pepper

1½ teaspoons vegetable oil

1 small onion, chopped fine

2 teaspoons all-purpose flour

1 teaspoon tomato paste

1¼ cups beef broth

3 tablespoons brandy

1 teaspoon soy sauce

1 teaspoon Dijon mustard

3 ounces (2 cups) wide egg noodles

¼ cup sour cream

1 tablespoon chopped fresh chives

1. Microwave mushrooms in covered bowl until volume has decreased by half and liquid is exuded, about 4 minutes. Drain mushrooms and set aside.

2. Pat beef dry with paper towels and season with salt and pepper. Heat oil in 10-inch skillet over medium heat until just smoking. Cook beef until well browned on all sides and meat registers 120 to 125 degrees (for medium-rare), 8 to 10 minutes, reducing heat if fond begins to burn. Transfer to plate. Add onion and mushrooms to now-empty skillet and cook until beginning to brown, 6 to 8 minutes. Stir in flour and tomato paste and cook for 1 minute.

3. Whisk in broth, brandy, soy sauce, mustard, and ¼ teaspoon pepper and bring to simmer, scraping up any browned bits. Add noodles and bring to boil. Cover, reduce heat to medium-low, and simmer, stirring occasionally, until noodles are tender and sauce is thickened, 8 to 10 minutes.

4. Meanwhile, slice beef against grain into ¼-inch-thick pieces. Stir beef and any accumulated juices into noodles and cover until warmed through, about 1 minute. Off heat, stir in sour cream and chives and season with salt and pepper to taste. Serve.

pan-roasted filets mignons with asparagus and garlic-herb butter

why this recipe works Filet mignon is the most tender steak there is—and it is also one of the most expensive. However, when you're buying only two, we think they are well worth the indulgence. We wanted a foolproof method for cooking filets that would ensure a deeply browned, rich crust and perfectly rosy interior every time. And while we were at it, we wanted to create an elegant but simple side dish that made use of the flavorful fond left in the pan by the steaks. The best way to cook the filets proved to be a dual method of starting with a sear on the stovetop and then transferring the skillet to the oven to finish cooking the steaks through. Since we wanted to make a side dish at the same time, however, we decided to preheat a baking sheet in the oven so we could transfer the steaks from the hot skillet to the sheet, freeing up the pan. Delicate, grassy asparagus readily picked up the savory flavor of the fond; arranging the spears carefully and covering them for part of the cooking time guaranteed that they came out evenly cooked and crisp-tender. A simple compound butter flavored with garlic and fresh herbs was an indulgent finishing touch to this date-night-worthy meal. Thick asparagus (about ½ inch thick at the base) works best in this recipe; do not use pencil-thin asparagus spears because they cannot withstand intense heat and will quickly overcook.

serves 2
total time: 45 minutes

3 tablespoons unsalted butter, softened

2 teaspoons minced fresh tarragon

2 teaspoons minced fresh parsley

1 garlic clove, minced

Salt and pepper

2 (6- to 8-ounce) center-cut filets mignons, 1½ inches thick, trimmed

2 teaspoons vegetable oil

1 pound asparagus, trimmed

1. Adjust oven rack to lower-middle position, place rimmed baking sheet on rack, and heat oven to 425 degrees. Combine 2 tablespoons butter, tarragon, parsley, garlic, ⅛ teaspoon salt, and ⅛ teaspoon pepper in bowl; set aside.

2. Pat steaks dry with paper towels and season with salt and pepper. Tie kitchen twine around middles of steaks. Heat oil in 10-inch skillet over medium-high heat until just smoking. Carefully place steaks in skillet and cook until well browned on both sides, about 6 minutes, flipping halfway through cooking.

3. Transfer steaks to baking sheet and bake until steaks register 120 to 125 degrees (for medium-rare), 10 to 15 minutes. Transfer steaks to plate, tent loosely with aluminum foil, and let rest for 5 minutes. Discard twine.

4. Meanwhile, melt remaining 1 tablespoon butter in now-empty skillet over medium heat. Add asparagus to skillet, arranging spears so that half of tips point in one direction and other half point in opposite direction. Cover and cook until asparagus is bright green and almost tender, 3 to 5 minutes.

5. Remove cover and season with salt and pepper. Increase heat to medium-high and continue to cook, turning spears, until spears are tender and well browned, 3 to 7 minutes. Transfer to platter. Evenly spoon garlic-herb butter over each steak and serve.

herb-crusted beef tenderloin

why this recipe works We love a showstopping beef tenderloin, but a typical roast serves 10 to 12 people. Could we scale it down for two without losing any of the appeal of this special dish? We knew that the best swap for a full-size beef tenderloin would be a couple of center-cut filets mignons, since these luxurious steaks are cut from the tenderloin. We started by giving the steaks a good sear in a skillet to deeply brown the exteriors; we then transferred them to a wire rack set in a rimmed baking sheet and topped them with an ultraflavorful herb paste (made with Parmesan cheese, chopped fresh parsley, olive oil, minced garlic, and thyme) as well as some panko bread crumbs, which lent great texture and crunch. Finishing the steaks in the oven allowed them to gently cook through to a perfect medium-rare.

serves 2
total time: 45 minutes

1 ounce Parmesan cheese, grated (½ cup)

¼ cup chopped fresh parsley

¼ cup extra-virgin olive oil

2 garlic cloves, minced

1 teaspoon chopped fresh thyme

Salt and pepper

2 (6- to 8-ounce) center-cut filets mignons, 1½ to 2 inches thick, trimmed

¼ cup panko bread crumbs

1. Adjust oven rack to middle position and heat oven to 450 degrees. Set wire rack in rimmed baking sheet. Process Parmesan, parsley, 3 tablespoons oil, garlic, thyme, ¼ teaspoon salt, and ¼ teaspoon pepper in food processor until smooth paste forms, about 10 seconds, scraping down sides of bowl as needed; set aside.

2. Pat steaks dry with paper towels and season with salt and pepper. Tie kitchen twine around middles of steaks. Heat remaining 1 tablespoon oil in 10-inch skillet over medium-high heat until just smoking. Cook steaks until well browned on both sides, about 3 minutes per side.

3. Transfer steaks to prepared wire rack. Spread 2 tablespoons herb paste on top of each steak, then top each with 2 tablespoons panko, pressing gently to adhere.

4. Roast until meat registers 120 to 125 degrees (for medium-rare), 14 to 16 minutes, rotating sheet halfway through roasting. Let steaks cool on wire rack for 5 minutes. Discard twine and serve.

steak au poivre with brandied cream sauce

why this recipe works At its best, steak au poivre features a slightly sweet and smooth sauce with hints of shallot and brandy that's a perfect counterpoint to the fiery pungency of the steak's peppercorn crust. For our scaled-down version, we started with beefy, well-marbled boneless strip steaks. For the peppercorn crust, cracked black peppercorns provided just the right balance of sharp bite, intense flavor, and subtle smokiness. To ensure that the heat from the peppercorns didn't overwhelm the dish, we opted to coat only one side of each steak. Pressing the steaks with a cake pan as they cooked guaranteed a good sear; this produced plenty of fond, which we used to develop a rich foundation of flavor for the accompanying sauce. Reserving a small amount of the brandy to stir into the sauce just before serving ensured that its flavor came through in the finished dish. Do not substitute finely ground pepper for the cracked peppercorns here.

serves 2
total time: 35 minutes

2 (8-ounce) boneless strip steaks, ¾ inch thick, trimmed

Salt and pepper

4 teaspoons black peppercorns, cracked

5 teaspoons vegetable oil

1 shallot, minced

1 teaspoon all-purpose flour

¾ cup chicken broth

3 tablespoons brandy

2 tablespoons heavy cream

2 tablespoons minced fresh chives

2 teaspoons lemon juice

½ teaspoon Dijon mustard

1. Pat steaks dry with paper towels and season with salt. Rub peppercorns evenly over 1 side of each steak and, using your fingers, press peppercorns into steaks to adhere.

2. Heat 1 tablespoon oil in 12-inch skillet over medium-high heat until just smoking. Place steaks, peppered side up, in skillet. Firmly press on steaks with bottom of cake pan and cook until well browned on first side, 3 to 5 minutes.

3. Flip steaks and reduce heat to medium. Firmly press on steaks with bottom of cake pan and continue to cook until meat registers 120 to 125 degrees (for medium-rare), 1 to 4 minutes longer; transfer to plate and tent with aluminum foil. Pour off fat from skillet and remove any stray peppercorns.

4. Heat remaining 2 teaspoons oil in now-empty skillet over medium heat until shimmering. Add shallot and cook until softened, about 2 minutes. Stir in flour and cook for 1 minute. Whisk in broth and 2 tablespoons brandy, scraping up any browned bits. Bring to simmer and cook until sauce is slightly thickened, 6 to 8 minutes.

5. Stir in cream and any accumulated meat juices and simmer for 30 seconds. Off heat, whisk in chives, lemon juice, mustard, and remaining 1 tablespoon brandy. Season with salt and pepper to taste. Serve steaks with sauce.

steak fajitas

why this recipe works For steak fajitas we could make any time of year—not just during grilling season—we moved the operation indoors. Pan-searing the steak over medium-high heat mimicked the caramelized exterior and crisp edges of grilled steak. Flank steak had great beefy flavor, and slicing it against the grain ensured that every bite was tender. Drizzling it with a squeeze of lime juice after cooking added the bright tang and flavor of a marinade in a fraction of the time. Bell pepper and onion are traditional accompaniments for fajitas; just one of each was plenty for our scaled-down recipe. Chili powder, cumin, and hot sauce added the smoky, spicy notes we wanted. To make these fajitas even spicier, add a sliced jalapeño with the bell pepper. Serve with your favorite fajita toppings.

serves 2
total time: 30 minutes

1 (12-ounce) flank steak, trimmed

Salt and pepper

2 tablespoons vegetable oil

1 tablespoon lime juice

1 red, green, or yellow bell pepper, stemmed, seeded, and cut into ½-inch-wide strips

1 small red onion, halved and sliced thin

2 tablespoons water

1 teaspoon chili powder

¼ teaspoon ground cumin

¼ teaspoon hot sauce

6 (6-inch) flour tortillas, warmed

1. Pat steak dry with paper towels and season with salt and pepper. Heat 1 tablespoon oil in 10-inch skillet over medium-high heat until just smoking. Lay steak in skillet and cook until well browned on first side, 3 to 5 minutes. Flip steak, reduce heat to medium, and continue to cook until meat registers 120 to 125 degrees (for medium-rare), 3 to 5 minutes; transfer to cutting board and drizzle with lime juice. Tent loosely with aluminum foil.

2. Heat remaining 1 tablespoon oil in now-empty skillet over medium heat until shimmering. Add bell pepper, onion, water, chili powder, cumin, hot sauce, and ¼ teaspoon salt. Cook, scraping up any browned bits, until vegetables are softened, 5 to 7 minutes; transfer to serving platter.

3. Slice steak thin against grain, arrange on platter with vegetables, and serve with warm tortillas.

thai-style beef salad

why this recipe works Traditionally, the steak for Thai-style beef salad is marinated for hours before cooking. We came up with a far quicker method: marinating the meat after cooking. After letting the steak rest, we sliced it and then tossed it with a tangy, Asian-inspired dressing. Meanwhile, we combined sliced onion and cucumber as well as some cilantro and mint with cooked rice noodles and more of the dressing. The salty dressing pulled moisture from the vegetables, so we drained the excess liquid from the mixture before combining it with the steak on a bed of lettuce and drizzling the salad with the remaining dressing. A garnish of chopped peanuts provided the perfect finishing touch. Do not substitute other types of noodles for the rice vermicelli here.

serves 2
total time: 45 minutes

2 ounces dried rice vermicelli

1 (8-ounce) flank steak, trimmed

Salt and pepper

3 tablespoons vegetable oil

3 tablespoons lime juice (2 limes)

3 tablespoons fish sauce

1 tablespoon packed brown sugar

1 small red onion, halved and sliced thin

½ cucumber, peeled, halved lengthwise, seeded, and sliced thin

2 teaspoons minced fresh cilantro

2 teaspoons minced fresh mint

½ head Bibb lettuce (4 ounces), leaves separated

2 tablespoons chopped dry-roasted peanuts

1. Bring 2 quarts water to boil in medium saucepan. Off heat, add noodles and let sit, stirring occasionally, until tender, about 10 minutes. Drain noodles, rinse with cold water, and drain again, leaving noodles slightly wet.

2. Meanwhile, pat steak dry with paper towels and season with salt and pepper. Heat 1 tablespoon oil in 10-inch skillet over medium-high heat until just smoking. Lay steak in skillet and cook until well browned on first side, 3 to 5 minutes. Flip steak, reduce heat to medium, and continue to cook until meat registers 120 to 125 degrees (for medium-rare), 3 to 5 minutes. Transfer steak to cutting board, tent loosely with aluminum foil, and let rest for 5 minutes.

3. Whisk remaining 2 tablespoons oil, lime juice, fish sauce, and sugar together in bowl until sugar dissolves. Slice steak in half lengthwise, then slice thin against grain. Toss sliced steak with 2 tablespoons dressing in separate bowl and let sit for 5 minutes. In third bowl, toss cooked noodles, onion, cucumber, cilantro, and mint with 3 tablespoons dressing and let sit for 5 minutes.

4. Divide lettuce leaves between two plates or arrange on serving platter. Drain noodle mixture and arrange over lettuce. Drain steak and arrange over salad. Drizzle with remaining dressing, sprinkle with peanuts, and serve.

beef stir-fry with bell peppers and black pepper sauce

why this recipe works We discovered that in order to produce a stir-fry with the type of velvety, tender beef normally found only in Chinese restaurants, we needed to choose the right cut of meat and treat it properly. Flank steak, cut against the grain into bite-size pieces, delivered great beef flavor and a moderate chew. A combination of meat tenderizing techniques—soaking the meat briefly in a mild baking soda solution and adding some cornstarch to the marinade before flash-searing it in a very hot pan—finished the job of delivering supertender, restaurant-quality beef stir-fry. Red and green bell peppers, along with some scallion greens, gave the dish great color and texture while keeping the focus on the beef. A generous amount of black pepper gave our sauce a bold kick and tied everything together. The vegetables and aromatics can be prepared while the beef is marinating. Serve with Simple White Rice (page 164).

serves 2
total time: 45 minutes

2 teaspoons plus 2 tablespoons water

⅛ teaspoon baking soda

8 ounces flank steak, trimmed, cut with grain into 2- to 2½-inch strips, each strip cut crosswise against grain into ¼-inch-thick slices

1½ tablespoons soy sauce

1½ tablespoons dry sherry or Chinese rice wine

1½ teaspoons cornstarch

1¼ teaspoons packed light brown sugar

1½ teaspoons oyster sauce

1 teaspoon rice vinegar

¾ teaspoon toasted sesame oil

1 teaspoon coarsely ground pepper

4 teaspoons vegetable oil

½ red bell pepper, cut into ¼-inch-wide strips

½ green bell pepper, cut into ¼-inch-wide strips

3 scallions, white parts sliced thin on bias, green parts cut into 2-inch pieces

2 garlic cloves, minced

2 teaspoons grated fresh ginger

1. Combine 2 teaspoons water and baking soda in medium bowl. Add beef and toss to coat. Let sit at room temperature for 5 minutes.

2. Whisk 1½ teaspoons soy sauce, 1½ teaspoons sherry, ¾ teaspoon cornstarch, and ¼ teaspoon sugar together in small bowl. Add soy sauce mixture to beef, stir to coat, and let sit at room temperature for 15 to 30 minutes.

3. Whisk remaining 2 tablespoons water, remaining 1 tablespoon soy sauce, remaining 1 tablespoon sherry, remaining ¾ teaspoon cornstarch, remaining 1 teaspoon sugar, oyster sauce, vinegar, sesame oil, and pepper together in second bowl.

4. Heat 1 teaspoon vegetable oil in 12-inch nonstick skillet over high heat until just smoking. Add beef in single layer. Cook without stirring for 1 minute. Continue to cook, stirring occasionally, until spotty brown on both sides, about 1 minute longer. Transfer to bowl.

5. Return now-empty skillet to high heat, add 1 teaspoon vegetable oil, and heat until just smoking. Add bell peppers and scallion greens and cook, stirring occasionally, until vegetables are spotty brown and crisp-tender, 2 to 3 minutes. Transfer vegetables to bowl with beef.

6. Return now-empty skillet to medium-high heat and add remaining 2 teaspoons vegetable oil, scallion whites, garlic, and ginger. Cook, stirring frequently, until lightly browned, 1 to 2 minutes. Return beef and vegetables to skillet and stir to combine.

7. Whisk sauce to recombine. Add to skillet and cook, stirring constantly, until sauce has thickened, about 30 seconds. Serve immediately.

thai red beef curry

why this recipe works Beef curry can be a satisfying meal for two on busy evenings, but takeout versions are often greasy and lack complex curry flavor. We sought a way to prepare this dish at home with little fuss but loads of flavor. Most of our beef recipes start with browning the meat to enhance and deepen the flavor of the dish. But in this curry, we found the distinct, bold flavors of curry paste, coconut milk, and fish sauce made the browning step unnecessary. Instead, we saved ourselves some time and simply slipped the beef into the simmering sauce and let it absorb the bold Thai flavors. Because the flank steak had already been cut into thin strips, it cooked through in just a few minutes. Crunchy bell pepper and sugar snap peas contributed fresh flavor and texture. Some basil and a splash of lime juice before serving brightened up the dish and tied everything together. Light coconut milk can be substituted for regular coconut milk, but the sauce will be slightly thinner. If you prefer your curry a little less spicy, reduce the amount of curry paste to 1 teaspoon.

serves 2
total time: 30 minutes

1½ teaspoons vegetable oil

2 teaspoons red curry paste

¾ cup canned coconut milk

1 tablespoon fish sauce

2 teaspoons packed light brown sugar

12 ounces flank steak, trimmed, cut into 2-inch-wide strips with grain, then sliced thin against grain

1 small red bell pepper, stemmed, seeded, and cut into ¼-inch-wide strips

4 ounces sugar snap peas, strings removed

½ cup coarsely chopped fresh basil

1 tablespoon lime juice

Salt

1. Heat oil in 12-inch skillet over medium heat until shimmering. Add curry paste and cook until fragrant, about 30 seconds. Whisk in coconut milk, fish sauce, and sugar and simmer until slightly thickened, about 5 minutes.

2. Add beef and cook until pieces separate and turn firm, 3 to 5 minutes. Stir in bell pepper and peas and cook until peas are crisp tender, about 5 minutes. Off heat, stir in basil and lime juice. Season with salt to taste, and serve.

spice-rubbed flank steak with spicy corn and black bean salad

why this recipe works We wanted a simple meal that would pair tender, well-seared steak with an easy, flavorful side. Flank steak was the ticket, but we found that the right cooking technique was the real key to success. We coated the steak with a flavorful spice rub before searing it, which contributed bold flavor, and we also heated the oil until just smoking to ensure a substantial, well-browned crust. A roasted corn and black bean salad was the perfect simple yet satisfying accompaniment to our steak; after toasting the corn in the skillet to bring out its natural sweetness and achieve some browning, we combined it with canned black beans, red bell pepper, jalapeño, a squeeze of lime juice, and a sprinkling of cilantro for a Southwestern-inspired meal we could enjoy any night of the week. Be sure to use fresh corn here; canned or frozen corn will not toast well.

serves 2
total time: 40 minutes

salad

1 teaspoon vegetable oil

1 ear corn, kernels cut from cob

¾ cup canned black beans, rinsed

1 red bell pepper, stemmed, seeded, and chopped fine

½ jalapeño chile, stemmed, seeded, and minced

2 tablespoons lime juice

2 tablespoons minced fresh cilantro

2 garlic cloves, minced

Salt and pepper

steak

½ teaspoon chili powder

½ teaspoon ground cumin

¼ teaspoon granulated garlic

¼ teaspoon salt

¼ teaspoon pepper

1 (1-pound) flank steak, trimmed

1 tablespoon vegetable oil

1. for the salad Heat oil in 10-inch nonstick skillet over medium-high heat until shimmering. Add corn and cook, without stirring, until well browned and toasted, 5 to 7 minutes. Transfer corn to medium bowl and let cool slightly. Wipe skillet clean.

2. Stir black beans, bell pepper, jalapeño, lime juice, cilantro, and garlic into toasted corn and season with salt and pepper to taste. Cover and refrigerate until flavors meld, about 15 minutes.

3. for the steak Meanwhile, combine chili powder, cumin, granulated garlic, salt, and pepper in separate bowl. Pat steak dry with paper towels, then rub spice mixture evenly over steak.

4. Heat oil in now-empty skillet over medium-high heat until just smoking. Lay steak in skillet and cook until well browned on first side, 3 to 5 minutes, reducing heat if spices begin to burn. Flip steak, reduce heat to medium, and continue to cook until meat registers 120 to 125 degrees (for medium-rare), 5 to 7 minutes. Transfer steak to cutting board, tent loosely with aluminum foil, and let rest for 5 minutes. Slice steak thin against grain. Serve with salad.

yankee pot roast

why this recipe works Yankee pot roast—a big piece of beef braised slowly with lots of onions, carrots, and potatoes—is a hearty one-pot dinner meant to feed a crowd. In a household of two, though, that same roast becomes a week's worth of boring repeat meals. We wanted a recipe that wouldn't leave us with days of leftovers—a scaled-down version featuring supertender meat and a full-flavored sauce. We started with beefy top blade steaks, which are nicely marbled. To ensure that our vegetables turned out tender, not mushy, we waited until the last hour of braising to add them. For the braising liquid, tasters favored chicken broth for its clean, savory flavor. Sautéed aromatics and a bit of tomato paste and soy sauce contributed depth of flavor that further enhanced the sauce. A dash of balsamic vinegar added at the end rounded out the sauce with a bit of acidity. If your skillet doesn't have a lid, use potholders to cover it with foil.

serves 2
total time: 2 hours 50 minutes

---

2 (8- to 10-ounce) beef top blade steaks, trimmed

Salt and pepper

4 teaspoons vegetable oil

3 carrots, peeled (½ carrot chopped fine, 2½ carrots cut into 1½-inch pieces)

1 onion (½ onion chopped fine, ½ onion cut into 4 wedges through root end)

1 celery rib, minced

2 garlic cloves, minced

2 teaspoons tomato paste

1¾ cups chicken broth

2 teaspoons soy sauce

1 sprig fresh thyme

1 bay leaf

10 ounces red potatoes, unpeeled, cut into 1-inch pieces

2 tablespoons minced fresh parsley

1 teaspoon balsamic vinegar

1. Adjust oven rack to middle position and heat oven to 325 degrees. Pat steaks dry with paper towels and season with salt and pepper.

2. Heat 2 teaspoons oil in 12-inch ovensafe skillet over medium-high heat until just smoking. Brown steaks on both sides, about 3 minutes per side; transfer to plate.

3. Reduce heat to medium, add remaining 2 teaspoons oil to now-empty skillet, and heat until shimmering. Add chopped carrot, chopped onion, celery, and ½ teaspoon salt and cook until golden, about 5 minutes. Stir in garlic and tomato paste and cook until fragrant, about 30 seconds. Stir in broth, soy sauce, thyme sprig, and bay leaf and bring to boil. Return steaks and any accumulated juices to skillet. Cover, transfer skillet to oven, and cook for 1¼ hours.

4. Flip steaks and add carrot pieces, onion wedges, and potatoes to skillet. Cover and cook until vegetables are tender and fork slips easily in and out of meat, 50 minutes to 1 hour.

5. Using slotted spoon, transfer steaks and vegetables to platter; tent with aluminum foil. Using large spoon, skim excess fat from surface of braising liquid; discard thyme sprig and bay leaf. Bring liquid to boil over medium-high heat and cook until reduced to 1 cup, about 3 minutes. Off heat, stir in parsley and vinegar. Season with salt and pepper to taste. Pour sauce over steaks and vegetables and serve.

teriyaki-glazed steak tips

why this recipe works We wanted to bring flavorful, juicy steak teriyaki to the table without having to head outside and fire up the grill for only two diners. For the meat, we settled on steak tips, which have lots of beefy flavor and cook quickly. Next, we made a simple teriyaki glaze with soy sauce, sugar, mirin, ginger, and garlic. Red pepper flakes provided a subtle kick, while a little cornstarch helped thicken the glaze to nicely coat the beef. Preparing the glaze right in the skillet we had just used to cook the steak not only made our recipe a one-pot affair, but the large surface area also allowed the glaze to reduce to a perfect, glossy consistency in record time. Steak tips, also known as flap meat, are sold as whole steak, cubes, and strips. To ensure evenly sized pieces, we prefer to purchase whole steak tips and cut them ourselves. Note that the cooking times may vary depending on the size of the steak tips. Serve with Simple White Rice (page 164).

serves 2
total time: 30 minutes

1 pound sirloin steak tips, trimmed and cut into 2-inch pieces

Pepper

1 tablespoon vegetable oil

¼ cup sugar

2 tablespoons soy sauce

1 tablespoon mirin, sweet sherry, or dry white wine

1 teaspoon grated fresh ginger

1 garlic clove, minced

¼ teaspoon cornstarch

Pinch red pepper flakes

2 scallions, sliced thin

1. Pat beef dry with paper towels and season with pepper. Heat oil in 10-inch skillet over medium-high heat until just smoking. Add beef and cook until well browned on all sides and meat registers 120 to 125 degrees (for medium-rare), 5 to 7 minutes; transfer to plate and tent loosely with aluminum foil. Pour off fat from skillet.

2. Meanwhile, whisk sugar, soy sauce, mirin, ginger, garlic, cornstarch, and pepper flakes together in bowl. Add soy sauce mixture to now-empty skillet, bring to simmer, and cook, stirring occasionally, until sauce is thick and glossy, about 2 minutes. Stir in any accumulated meat juices and simmer for 30 seconds. Return browned steak tips to skillet and turn to coat with sauce. Sprinkle with scallions and serve.

juicy pub-style burgers

why this recipe works Few things are as satisfying as a thick, juicy pub-style burger. But avoiding the usual gray band of overcooked meat is a challenge. We wanted a patty that was well-seared, juicy, and evenly rosy from center to edge. Grinding our own meat in the food processor was a must for this ultimate burger, and sirloin steak tips were the right cut for the job. Cutting the meat into small chunks before grinding and lightly packing it to form patties gave the burgers just enough structure to hold their shape in the skillet. A little melted butter improved their flavor and juiciness, but our biggest discovery came when we transferred the burgers from the stovetop to the oven to finish cooking: The stovetop provided intense heat for searing, while the oven's ambient heat allowed for even cooking—thus eliminating the overcooked gray zone. Steak tips, also known as flap meat, are sold as whole steak, cubes, and strips; look for either whole steak tips or strips that are easy to cut into small pieces for this recipe. When stirring the butter and pepper into the ground meat and shaping the patties, take care not to overwork the meat, or the burgers will be dense. Serve with your favorite burger toppings.

serves 2
total time: 1 hour

1 pound sirloin steak tips, trimmed and cut into ½-inch pieces

2 tablespoons unsalted butter, melted and cooled

Salt and pepper

1 teaspoon vegetable oil

¼ cup mayonnaise

2 teaspoons soy sauce

2 teaspoons minced fresh chives

1 teaspoon packed brown sugar

¾ teaspoon Worcestershire sauce

1 small garlic clove, minced

2 large hamburger buns, toasted and buttered

1. Place beef on rimmed baking sheet in single layer. Freeze beef until very firm and starting to harden around edges but still pliable, about 25 minutes.

2. Pulse half of beef in food processor until finely ground into ¹⁄₁₆-inch pieces, about 35 pulses, scraping down sides of bowl as needed to ensure that beef is evenly ground. Return ground beef to empty side of sheet. Repeat with remaining half of beef; return to sheet. Spread ground beef on sheet and inspect carefully, removing any long strands of gristle and large chunks of hard meat or fat.

3. Adjust oven rack to middle position and heat oven to 300 degrees. Drizzle melted butter over ground beef and add ½ teaspoon pepper. Gently toss with fork to combine, being careful not to overwork meat. Divide meat mixture into 2 lightly packed balls, then gently flatten each ball into ¾-inch-thick patty.

4. Season patties with salt and pepper. Heat oil in 10-inch skillet over high heat until just smoking. Using spatula, place burgers in skillet and cook without moving for 2 minutes. Flip burgers and continue to cook for 2 minutes. Transfer patties to clean, dry rimmed baking sheet and bake until burgers register 120 to 125 degrees (for medium-rare), 3 to 6 minutes. Transfer burgers to plate and let rest for 5 minutes.

5. Whisk mayonnaise, soy sauce, chives, sugar, Worcestershire, garlic, and ¼ teaspoon pepper together in bowl. Serve burgers on buns with sauce.

classic lasagna

why this recipe works Lasagna is a crowd-pleaser: What's not to love about a dish featuring layers of tender noodles, meaty sauce, and gooey cheese that's baked until golden and bubbling? But it's also time-consuming to prepare. We didn't think this hearty and satisfying favorite should be off-limits when cooking for less than a crowd, so we set our sights on a streamlined version for two. Our first task was to develop an easy sauce. We found that meatloaf mix lent more flavor and richness than ground beef alone. A little cream added to diced tomatoes and canned tomato sauce gave us a velvety sauce reminiscent of a Bolognese. We hoped to avoid the time-consuming step of boiling lasagna noodles; luckily, we found success using no-boil noodles. Our last concern was the baking vessel: The usual baking dish holds far too much lasagna for two, but the right amount of noodles fit perfectly in a loaf pan. We simply layered the noodles with the sauce and a combination of three cheeses: mozzarella, ricotta, and Parmesan. We baked the lasagna covered for part of the cooking time so the noodles could fully tenderize, then uncovered it to brown the top. What emerged was a beautiful, bubbling, perfectly proportioned two-person lasagna. If you can't find meatloaf mix, substitute equal parts ground pork and 90 percent lean ground beef. Either whole-milk or part-skim ricotta will work, but do not substitute fat-free ricotta.

serves 2
total time: 1 hour 40 minutes

sauce
1 tablespoon extra-virgin olive oil

1 small onion, chopped fine

Salt and pepper

2 garlic cloves, minced

8 ounces meatloaf mix

2 tablespoons heavy cream

1 (14.5-ounce) can diced tomatoes, drained with ¼ cup juice reserved

1 (8-ounce) can tomato sauce

filling, noodles, and cheese
4 ounces (½ cup) whole-milk or part-skim ricotta cheese

1 ounce Parmesan cheese, grated (½ cup), plus 2 tablespoons grated

3 tablespoons chopped fresh basil

1 large egg, lightly beaten

⅛ teaspoon salt

⅛ teaspoon pepper

4 no-boil lasagna noodles

4 ounces whole-milk mozzarella cheese, shredded (1 cup)

1. **for the sauce** Adjust oven rack to middle position and heat oven to 400 degrees. Heat oil in large saucepan over medium heat until shimmering. Add onion and ⅛ teaspoon salt and cook until softened, about 5 minutes. Stir in garlic and cook until fragrant, about 30 seconds. Stir in meatloaf mix and cook, breaking up meat with wooden spoon, until no longer pink, about 2 minutes. Stir in cream, bring to simmer, and cook until liquid evaporates, about 2 minutes. Stir in tomatoes and reserved juice and tomato sauce. Bring to simmer and cook until flavors are blended, about 2 minutes. Season with salt and pepper to taste.

2. **for the filling, noodles, and cheese** Combine ricotta, ½ cup Parmesan, basil, egg, salt, and pepper in bowl.

3. Spread ½ cup sauce over bottom of loaf pan, avoiding large chunks of meat. Lay 1 noodle in pan, spread one-third of ricotta mixture over noodle, sprinkle with ¼ cup mozzarella, and top with ½ cup sauce; repeat layering 2 more times. Lay remaining noodle in pan and top with remaining sauce, remaining ¼ cup mozzarella, and remaining 2 tablespoons Parmesan.

4. Cover pan tightly with aluminum foil that has been sprayed with vegetable oil spray. Bake until sauce bubbles lightly around edges, 25 to 30 minutes. Remove foil and continue to bake until hot throughout and cheese is browned in spots, about 10 minutes longer. Let cool for 20 minutes before serving.

spaghetti bolognese

why this recipe works Bolognese is usually reserved for weekends at home, when a big pot of the aromatic, long-simmering sauce means Sunday supper with the family. But we think its comforts shouldn't be out of reach on busy weeknights with just two to feed. Our challenges were to downsize the yield, simplify the procedure, keep everything in balance, and produce a complex-tasting sauce—all in a fraction of the time. Meatloaf mix—a combination of ground beef, pork, and veal—balanced our sauce. Adding pancetta, dried porcini mushrooms, and anchovies to the classic onions and carrots was a quick and easy way to boost meaty, savory flavor. A can of diced tomatoes and a bit of milk gave our sauce just the right acidity and richness. As an added bonus, we found we could make this a one-pot meal by cooking the spaghetti right in the sauce; adding a bit of water ensured that the pasta had enough liquid to absorb. If you can't find meatloaf mix, substitute equal parts 85 percent lean ground beef and ground pork. Serve with grated Parmesan cheese.

serves 2
total time: 1 hour 15 minutes

1 small onion, chopped coarse

1 carrot, peeled and chopped coarse

1½ ounces pancetta, chopped coarse

¼ ounce dried porcini mushrooms, rinsed

1 anchovy fillet, rinsed

1 (14.5-ounce) can diced tomatoes

1 tablespoon unsalted butter

1 tablespoon tomato paste

2 garlic cloves, minced

½ teaspoon sugar

⅛ teaspoon red pepper flakes

6 ounces meatloaf mix

¾ cup whole milk

¼ cup dry white wine

2 cups water

6 ounces spaghetti

2 tablespoons chopped fresh basil

Salt and pepper

1. Pulse onion, carrot, pancetta, mushrooms, and anchovy in food processor until finely ground, 10 to 15 pulses; transfer to bowl. Pulse tomatoes and their juice until coarsely ground, about 8 pulses.

2. Melt butter in 12-inch nonstick skillet over medium heat. Add onion mixture and cook until browned, 6 to 8 minutes. Stir in tomato paste, garlic, sugar, and pepper flakes and cook until paste begins to darken, about 1 minute. Add meatloaf mix, breaking up meat with wooden spoon, and cook until no longer pink, 2 to 3 minutes.

3. Stir in milk and bring to simmer, scraping up any browned bits. Cook until liquid is nearly evaporated, 5 to 8 minutes. Stir in wine, bring to simmer, and cook until liquid is nearly evaporated, 2 to 3 minutes.

4. Add water, pasta, and processed tomatoes and bring to boil. Cover, reduce heat to medium, and simmer, stirring occasionally, until pasta is tender and sauce is thickened, 15 to 18 minutes. Off heat, stir in basil and season with salt and pepper to taste. Serve.

classic pork ragu

why this recipe works Featuring tender, shredded meat in a rich tomato sauce, classic pork ragu is a rustic alternative to more complicated meat sauces and delivers big, meaty flavor without a lot of work. Determining the right cut of pork for a scaled-down ragu was our biggest challenge, since many of the most flavorful cuts of pork are also the largest. Country-style ribs proved ideal; they are available in smaller portions and have plenty of fat and connective tissue to keep the meat moist during the long cooking time. Slowly simmered with a can of whole tomatoes and flavored with shallot, garlic, rosemary, and red wine, these meaty ribs delivered plenty of rich, savory flavor. Pork spareribs can be substituted for the country-style ribs. To prevent a greasy sauce, trim all external fat from the ribs before browning. Other pasta shapes can be substituted for the ziti; however, their cup measurements may vary.

serves 2
total time: 2 hours 15 minutes

1 (28-ounce) can whole peeled tomatoes, drained with ¼ cup juice reserved

12 ounces bone-in country-style pork ribs, trimmed

Salt and pepper

2 teaspoons extra-virgin olive oil

1 large shallot, minced

2 garlic cloves, minced

1½ teaspoons minced fresh rosemary

½ cup dry red wine

6 ounces (2 cups) ziti

Grated Pecorino Romano cheese

1. Pulse tomatoes in food processor until coarsely chopped and no large pieces remain, 6 to 8 pulses.

2. Pat pork dry with paper towels and season with salt and pepper. Heat oil in 10-inch skillet over medium-high heat until just smoking. Brown pork well on all sides, 8 to 10 minutes; transfer to plate.

3. Add shallot and ¼ teaspoon salt to fat left in skillet and cook over medium heat until softened, 2 to 3 minutes. Stir in garlic and rosemary and cook until fragrant, about 30 seconds. Stir in wine, scraping up any browned bits. Bring to simmer and cook until reduced by half, about 2 minutes.

4. Stir in tomatoes and reserved juice. Nestle browned ribs into sauce, along with any accumulated juices, and bring to simmer. Reduce heat to low, cover, and simmer gently, turning ribs occasionally, until meat is very tender and falling off bones, about 1½ hours.

5. Transfer ribs to plate, let cool slightly, then shred into bite-size pieces using 2 forks, discarding fat and bones. Return shredded meat to sauce, bring to simmer, and cook until heated through and slightly thickened, 2 to 3 minutes. Season with salt and pepper to taste.

6. Meanwhile, bring 4 quarts water to boil in large pot. Add pasta and 1 tablespoon salt and cook, stirring often, until al dente. Reserve ½ cup cooking water, then drain pasta and return it to pot. Add sauce and toss to combine. Season with salt and pepper to taste, and adjust consistency with reserved cooking water as needed. Serve with Pecorino.

pasta with beans, chard, and rosemary

why this recipe works Pasta, beans, and greens come together in a satisfying combination of flavors and textures for this rustic one-dish meal. Creamy cannellini beans (or meaty pinto beans) contributed plenty of heft and substance, and Swiss chard made an appealing twofer for the greens component: We sautéed the chopped chard stems at the outset of cooking but waited until the end to sprinkle the tender leaves on top, allowing them to steam gently off heat. A small amount of pancetta provided a meaty background, and two additions of rosemary gave the dish a subtle but pervasive herbal flavor. Instead of draining and rinsing the canned beans, we mixed the starchy liquid with water and a handful of grated Parmesan to produce a creamy, stew-like sauce that brought the dish together. We cooked the pasta separately until just shy of al dente and then finished cooking it in the broth so it could soak up some of the broth's meaty flavor. The sauce will thicken as it cools.

serves 2
total time: 45 minutes

1 tablespoon vegetable oil

1½ ounces pancetta, diced

½ onion, chopped fine

5 ounces Swiss chard, stems chopped fine, leaves chopped coarse

1 teaspoon minced fresh rosemary

½ teaspoon garlic, minced to paste

Pinch red pepper flakes

1 (15-ounce) can cannellini and/ or pinto beans (do not drain)

Parmesan cheese rind (optional), plus ½ ounce Parmesan cheese, grated (¼ cup), plus extra for serving

4 ounces (1¼ cups) fusilli

Salt

1½ teaspoons red wine vinegar

1. Heat oil in large saucepan over medium-high heat until just smoking. Add pancetta and cook, stirring occasionally, until pancetta begins to brown, 1 to 2 minutes. Stir in onion and chard stems and cook, stirring occasionally, until slightly softened, about 3 minutes. Add ½ teaspoon rosemary, garlic, and pepper flakes and cook until fragrant, about 1 minute. Stir in beans and their liquid, ¾ cup water, and Parmesan rind, if using, and bring to boil. Reduce heat to medium-low and simmer for 10 minutes.

2. Meanwhile, bring 2 quarts water to boil in medium saucepan. Add pasta and 1½ teaspoons salt and cook until pasta is just shy of al dente. Drain. Stir pasta into beans and spread chard leaves on top. Cover, remove from heat, and let sit until pasta is fully cooked and chard leaves are wilted, 5 to 7 minutes. Discard Parmesan rind, if using. Stir in remaining ½ teaspoon rosemary, ¼ cup Parmesan, and vinegar. Season with salt to taste, and serve, passing extra Parmesan separately.

orecchiette with broccoli rabe and italian sausage

why this recipe works The Italian region of Puglia is known for its simple, rustic cuisine. We wanted to create a version of one popular dish that features orecchiette paired with bitter broccoli rabe and sweet Italian sausage—and we wanted just enough to yield a comforting yet elegant dinner for two. Boiling the broccoli rabe allowed the stalks to become tender without overcooking the florets—and as a bonus, we were able to use the richly flavored water to cook the pasta. Browning the sausage provided a good flavor base for the sauce. Chicken broth plus garlic and red pepper flakes contributed a rich backbone, and just one minced anchovy fillet deepened the overall flavor of the dish. A little flour thickened our sauce to the proper luxurious consistency. Other pasta shapes can be substituted for the orecchiette; however, their cup measurements may vary. Don't confuse broccoli rabe with broccoli or broccolini; broccoli rabe is a member of the turnip family and has a peppery bite. Chicory or turnip greens can be substituted for the broccoli rabe.

serves 2
total time: 45 minutes

2 tablespoons extra-virgin olive oil

8 ounces sweet Italian sausage, casings removed

3 garlic cloves, minced

1 anchovy fillet, rinsed, patted dry, and minced

1 teaspoon all-purpose flour

¼ teaspoon red pepper flakes

¾ cup chicken broth

8 ounces broccoli rabe, trimmed and cut into 1½-inch pieces

Salt

6 ounces (1¾ cups) orecchiette

¼ cup grated Pecorino Romano cheese, plus extra for serving

1. Heat oil in 12-inch nonstick skillet over medium-high heat until shimmering. Add sausage and cook, breaking up meat with wooden spoon, until browned and crispy, 5 to 7 minutes.

2. Stir in garlic, anchovy, flour, and pepper flakes and cook until fragrant, about 30 seconds. Stir in broth, scraping up any browned bits. Bring to simmer and cook, stirring occasionally, until sauce is slightly thickened, about 1 minute. Remove from heat and cover to keep warm.

3. Meanwhile, bring 4 quarts water to boil in large pot. Add broccoli rabe and 1 tablespoon salt and cook, stirring often, until broccoli rabe turns bright green, about 2 minutes. Using slotted spoon, transfer broccoli rabe to paper towel–lined plate.

4. Return pot of water to boil. Add pasta and cook, stirring often, until al dente.

5. Reserve ½ cup cooking water, then drain pasta and return it to pot. Return sausage mixture to simmer. Add sausage mixture, broccoli rabe, and Pecorino to pasta and toss to combine. Adjust consistency with reserved cooking water as needed and season with salt to taste. Serve, passing extra Pecorino separately.

variation

orecchiette with broccoli rabe and white beans

Omit sausage and anchovy. Increase amount of garlic to 4 cloves and substitute vegetable broth for chicken broth. Add ¾ cup rinsed canned cannellini beans to skillet with broth. Add 2 tablespoons toasted pine nuts and 1½ teaspoons red wine vinegar to pasta with sauce in step 5.

glazed grilled pork chops with sweet potatoes

why this recipe works When cooking for two, firing up the grill is an easy option, and pork chops are an ideal, perfectly portioned choice. We opted for well-marbled rib chops and set up a two-level fire for grilling, which allowed us to sear the chops on the hotter side and then let them finish cooking gently over the cooler side. Covering the chops with foil after brushing on some glaze prevented them from drying out. To complete the meal, we parcooked sweet potatoes in the microwave before grilling them and tossing them in a light vinaigrette. If the pork is enhanced (injected with a salt solution), do not brine. If brining the pork, do not season the chops with salt in step 3.

serves 2
total time: 1 hour 30 minutes

sweet potatoes
¼ cup extra-virgin olive oil

2 tablespoons chopped fresh tarragon

1 tablespoon balsamic vinegar

1 small shallot, minced

Salt and pepper

Pinch sugar

2 small sweet potatoes (8 ounces each), unpeeled, halved lengthwise

pork chops
2 tablespoons maple syrup

2 tablespoons Dijon mustard

2 tablespoons whole-grain mustard

2 tablespoons extra-virgin olive oil

Pinch cayenne pepper

Salt and pepper

2 (8- to 10-ounce) bone-in rib or center-cut pork chops, ¾ to 1 inch thick, trimmed and brined if desired (see page 169)

1. for the sweet potatoes Whisk 3 tablespoons oil, tarragon, vinegar, shallot, ¼ teaspoon salt, ⅛ teaspoon pepper, and sugar together in medium bowl. Set aside.

2. Brush potato halves with remaining 1 tablespoon oil and season with salt. Arrange potatoes cut side down on plate and microwave until soft, 6 to 8 minutes, flipping halfway through microwaving.

3. for the pork chops Combine syrup, mustards, oil, cayenne, pinch salt, and pinch pepper in small bowl. Set aside ¼ cup glaze. Cut 2 slits, about 2 inches apart, through outer layer of fat and silverskin on each chop. Pat chops dry with paper towels and season with salt and pepper.

4a. for a charcoal grill Open bottom vent completely. Light large chimney starter filled with charcoal briquettes (6 quarts). When top coals are partially covered with ash, pour two-thirds evenly over half of grill, then pour remaining coals over other half of grill. Set cooking grate in place, cover, and open lid vent completely. Heat grill until hot, about 5 minutes.

4b. for a gas grill Turn all burners to high, cover, and heat grill until hot, about 15 minutes. Leave primary burner on high and turn other burner(s) to medium.

5. Clean and oil cooking grate. Place chops on hotter side of grill and cook until well browned on both sides, 6 to 10 minutes, flipping halfway through cooking.

6. Meanwhile, place potatoes cut side down on cooler side of grill. Cook until well browned, 18 to 20 minutes, flipping halfway through cooking.

7. Slide chops to cooler side of grill, brush with remaining glaze, and tent loosely with aluminum foil. Cover and continue to cook until meat registers 145 degrees, 5 to 10 minutes, flipping and brushing with glaze halfway through cooking. Transfer to platter, tent loosely with foil, and let rest for 5 to 10 minutes.

8. Transfer potatoes to cutting board and cut into 1-inch pieces. Whisk vinaigrette to recombine, then add potatoes to bowl and toss to coat. Transfer to platter with chops and serve, passing reserved glaze separately.

sautéed pork chops with pears and blue cheese

why this recipe works We wanted to create an elegant dinner for two featuring sautéed pork chops for a sophisticated yet unfussy meal. The mild sweetness of caramelized pears and the pungent flavor of blue cheese provided a perfect foil for our rich, savory chops and offered a welcome balance of flavors and textures. We found that bone-in chops were the best choice for this recipe: The bone ensured that the meat stayed juicy and moist. A dual-heat approach—searing one side over medium-high heat and then turning down the heat to cook the second side—allowed the chops to develop nice browning without overcooking. Once the chops were cooked, we set them aside to rest and combined chicken broth, butter, and balsamic vinegar for a simple pan sauce that complemented our dish without overwhelming the other flavors. Bosc pears, a firm, russet-colored variety, work best in this recipe. For the boldest flavor, make sure to use an assertive blue cheese such as Gorgonzola or Roquefort. If the pork is enhanced (injected with a salt solution), do not brine. If brining the pork, do not season with salt in step 1. Serve with Parmesan Polenta (page 165) or Basic Green Salad (page 169).

serves 2
total time: 45 minutes

2 (8- to 10-ounce) bone-in rib or center-cut pork chops, ¾ to 1 inch thick, trimmed and brined if desired (see page 169)

Salt and pepper

2 teaspoons vegetable oil

1 pear, halved, cored, and cut into ¾-inch-thick wedges

½ teaspoon sugar

¾ cup chicken broth

2 tablespoons unsalted butter, chilled

2 teaspoons balsamic vinegar

1 ounce blue cheese, crumbled (¼ cup)

1. Cut 2 slits, about 2 inches apart, through outer layer of fat and silverskin on each chop. Pat chops dry with paper towels and season with salt and pepper.

2. Heat 1 teaspoon oil in 10-inch skillet over medium-high heat until just smoking. Place chops in skillet and cook until well browned on first side, about 3 minutes. Flip chops, reduce heat to medium, and continue to cook until meat registers 145 degrees, 5 to 10 minutes longer; transfer to serving platter and tent with aluminum foil.

3. Toss pear wedges with sugar, ¼ teaspoon salt, and ⅛ teaspoon pepper in bowl. Heat remaining 1 teaspoon oil in now-empty skillet over medium-high heat until shimmering.

4. Place pear wedges cut side down in skillet and cook until golden brown on both sides, 1 to 2 minutes per side. Stir in broth, scraping up any browned bits. Bring to simmer and cook until pears are softened, about 5 minutes. Transfer pears to platter with chops.

5. Stir any accumulated meat juices into sauce and simmer until slightly thickened, 1 to 2 minutes. Off heat, whisk in butter and vinegar and season with salt and pepper to taste. Pour sauce over chops and pear wedges, sprinkle with blue cheese, and serve.

easiest-ever pulled pork

why this recipe works Most recipes for pulled pork yield enough tender, smoky meat to share with 10 or 12 of your closest friends; they also require plenty of time and patience. We wanted a pulled pork recipe for a party of two, and we wanted an easier approach—one that wouldn't require tending the grill all day. We started by bringing the cooking process indoors in hopes of finding a way to hurry up the proceedings. We knew we'd need a smaller cut than the traditional pork shoulder if we wanted to reduce both the yield and the time investment. We settled on bone-in blade chops, which produced tender, richly flavored meat that, once shredded, closely resembled classic barbecue; two 8- to 10-ounce bone-in blade-cut chops yielded just the right amount of meat. While roasting dried out the pork, braising showed promise. To infuse the meat with even more flavor, we cut the chops off the bone and into strips, which provided more surface area for our rub to cling to. We then browned the chops in a large saucepan and then moved them to a plate so we could build a classic barbecue sauce right in the same pan. Ketchup, cider vinegar, and brown sugar did the trick. After returning the pork to the sauce, we added some water, covered the pot, and slid it into the oven. About an hour and a half later, the meat was tender, shreddable, and full of flavor. It is important to trim away any large sections of fat to prevent the final dish from being overly greasy. Serve with dill pickle chips and coleslaw.

serves 2
total time: 2 hours 10 minutes

2 (8- to 10-ounce) bone-in blade-cut pork chops, ¾ to 1 inch thick

1 tablespoon packed brown sugar

1½ teaspoons paprika

½ teaspoon ground cumin

Salt and pepper

4 teaspoons vegetable oil

1 small onion, chopped fine

1 slice bacon, chopped fine

1 garlic clove, minced

⅛ teaspoon red pepper flakes

¼ cup cider vinegar

2 tablespoons ketchup

2 hamburger buns

1. Adjust oven rack to lower-middle position and heat oven to 300 degrees. Using sharp chef's knife, cut pork from bone, keeping knife as close to bone as possible. Trim any large sections of fat, then slice chops into 1-inch-thick strips.

2. Combine 1 teaspoon sugar, paprika, cumin, ¼ teaspoon salt, and ½ teaspoon pepper in bowl. Pat pork pieces dry with paper towels and rub with spice mixture.

3. Heat 2 teaspoons oil in large ovensafe saucepan over medium-high heat until just smoking. Add half of pork and brown on all sides, 1 to 3 minutes; transfer to plate. Repeat with remaining 2 teaspoons oil and remaining pork; transfer to plate.

4. Reduce heat to medium. Add onion and bacon to fat left in saucepan and cook until onion is softened, about 5 minutes. Add garlic and pepper flakes and cook until fragrant, about 30 seconds. Add vinegar, ketchup, and remaining 2 teaspoons sugar, scraping up any browned bits, and bring to simmer. Return pork and any accumulated juices to saucepan. Cover, transfer saucepan to oven, and cook until pork is tender, about 1½ hours.

5. Transfer pork to carving board, let cool slightly, and shred into bite-size pieces. Return pork and any accumulated juices to saucepan and toss to coat with sauce. Serve on buns.

crispy sesame pork chops with wilted napa cabbage salad

why this recipe works For simple pan-fried pork chops with an Asian-inspired twist, we coated them in crisp panko bread crumbs as well as sesame seeds, which added nutty flavor and even more crunch to the coating. Using a generous ⅓ cup of oil to fry the chops ensured that they developed a thoroughly crisp and golden brown crust. To round out the meal, we tossed together an easy cabbage slaw; briefly wilting the cabbage softened it to the perfect crisp-tender texture while the heat allowed the flavors of fragrant garlic, ginger, and rice vinegar to really bloom. If the pork is enhanced (injected with a salt solution), do not brine. If brining the pork, do not season with salt in step 2. Don't let the pork chops drain on the paper towels for longer than 30 seconds, or the heat will steam the crust and make it soggy.

serves 2
total time: 40 minutes

¼ cup all-purpose flour

1 large egg

⅔ cup panko bread crumbs

⅓ cup sesame seeds

4 (3– to 4-ounce) boneless pork chops, ½ to ¾ inch thick, trimmed and brined if desired (see page 169)

Salt and pepper

1½ tablespoons plus ⅓ cup vegetable oil

1½ teaspoons toasted sesame oil

1 garlic clove, minced

½ teaspoon grated fresh ginger

½ small head napa cabbage, cored and shredded (4 cups)

1 carrot, peeled and shredded

1 tablespoon rice vinegar, plus extra for seasoning

1. Set wire rack in rimmed baking sheet. Spread flour in shallow dish. Beat egg in second shallow dish. Combine panko and sesame seeds in third shallow dish.

2. Pat chops dry with paper towels and season with salt and pepper. Working with 1 chop at a time, dredge chops in flour, dip in egg, then coat with panko mixture, pressing gently to adhere; transfer to prepared rack.

3. Heat 1½ tablespoons vegetable oil and sesame oil in 12-inch nonstick skillet over medium heat until shimmering. Add garlic and ginger and cook until fragrant, about 30 seconds. Stir in cabbage and carrot and cook until just wilted, about 1 minute. Off heat, add vinegar and toss to combine. Transfer to serving bowl and season with salt, pepper, and extra vinegar to taste. Wipe skillet clean.

4. Line large plate with triple layer of paper towels. Heat remaining ⅓ cup vegetable oil in 12-inch nonstick skillet over medium-high heat until shimmering. Carefully lay chops in skillet and cook until golden brown and crisp on both sides and meat registers 145 degrees, 2 to 5 minutes per side. Drain chops briefly on paper towel–lined plate. Serve with cabbage salad.

bacon-wrapped pork chops with roasted potatoes

why this recipe works Baked pork chops couldn't be easier, but the results are often disappointing—all that dry heat usually results in dry meat. We wanted tender and juicy baked chops paired with a flavorful side dish. To keep our chops moist, we wrapped them in bacon; the fat from the bacon melted as it cooked, basting our chops and adding a subtle smoky flavor as well as juiciness. Microwaving the bacon for a few minutes gave it a jump start by allowing some of the fat to render, then we finished the chops under the broiler to crisp the bacon. Cooking the pork chops on a baking sheet made it easy to roast some potatoes alongside. If you can't find red potatoes measuring less than 1 inch in diameter, you can substitute larger red potatoes cut into ¾-inch chunks. The bacon should completely cover the top of the pork chops. If your bacon is narrow, you may need three slices per chop. If the pork is enhanced (injected with a salt solution), do not brine. If brining the pork, do not season with salt in step 3.

serves 2
total time: 1 hour

12 ounces extra-small red potatoes, unpeeled, halved

2 tablespoons extra-virgin olive oil

Salt and pepper

4–6 slices bacon

2 (6- to 8-ounce) boneless pork chops, ¾ to 1 inch thick, trimmed and brined if desired (see page 169)

1 teaspoon ground fennel

1 tablespoon minced fresh parsley

1. Adjust oven rack to upper-middle position and heat oven to 375 degrees. Line rimmed baking sheet with aluminum foil. Toss potatoes with 1 tablespoon oil and season with salt and pepper. Lay potatoes cut side down on half of prepared sheet and roast until just tender, about 20 minutes.

2. Meanwhile, lay bacon on large plate and weigh it down with second plate. Microwave bacon until slightly shriveled but still pliable, 1 to 3 minutes. Transfer bacon to paper towel–lined plate and let cool slightly.

3. Pat chops dry with paper towels, rub evenly with fennel, and season with salt and pepper. Shingle 2 or 3 slices of bacon lengthwise over top of each pork chop so each chop is covered, tucking ends underneath to secure.

4. Remove potatoes from oven, arrange pork tucked side down on empty half of sheet, and roast until pork registers 135 degrees, 12 to 15 minutes.

5. Remove pork and potatoes from oven, adjust oven rack 6 inches from broiler element, and heat broiler. Broil pork and potatoes until bacon is crisp and browned and meat registers 145 degrees, 2 to 4 minutes. Transfer pork to large plate, tent loosely with foil, and let rest for 5 minutes.

6. While chops rest, whisk remaining 1 tablespoon oil and parsley together in large bowl. Add potatoes and toss to coat. Season with salt and pepper to taste. Serve chops with potatoes.

maple-glazed pork tenderloin

why this recipe works Maple-glazed pork tenderloin is a New England tradition—and since a small tenderloin is just enough for two, we knew it would be a perfect addition to our scaled-down repertoire. Searing the meat gave it a flavorful browned exterior and created a fond we could use to build our glaze. Maple syrup, mustard, cider vinegar, a little bourbon, and a pinch of cayenne provided a balanced glaze with sweet, smoky, tart, and spicy notes. A sugar-and-cornstarch coating created a rough exterior to which the glaze could adhere so that every bite had plenty of maple flavor. Don't substitute imitation maple syrup—it will be too sweet. If the pork is enhanced (injected with a salt solution), do not brine. If brining the pork, omit the salt in step 2. Be sure to pat off the cornstarch mixture thoroughly in step 2, as any excess will leave gummy spots on the tenderloin.

serves 2
total time: 45 minutes

⅓ cup plus 1 tablespoon maple syrup

2 tablespoons whole-grain mustard

1 tablespoon bourbon

2 teaspoons cider vinegar

Salt and pepper

Pinch cayenne pepper

1 tablespoon cornstarch

1 teaspoon sugar

1 (12-ounce) pork tenderloin, trimmed and brined if desired (see page 169)

2 teaspoons vegetable oil

1. Adjust oven rack to middle position and heat oven to 350 degrees. Stir ⅓ cup maple syrup, mustard, bourbon, vinegar, ¼ teaspoon salt, and cayenne together in small bowl.

2. Combine cornstarch, sugar, ¼ teaspoon salt, and ¼ teaspoon pepper in shallow dish. Pat tenderloin dry with paper towels, then roll in cornstarch mixture until evenly coated on all sides; thoroughly pat off excess cornstarch mixture.

3. Heat oil in 10-inch ovensafe nonstick skillet over medium-high heat until just smoking. Brown tenderloin well on all sides, 6 to 8 minutes; transfer to plate.

4. Pour off fat from skillet and return to medium heat. Add syrup mixture to now-empty skillet, bring to simmer, scraping up any browned bits, and cook until reduced to ⅓ cup, 30 seconds to 1 minute. Return browned tenderloin to skillet and turn to coat with glaze. Transfer skillet to oven and roast tenderloin until meat registers 145 degrees, 8 to 12 minutes.

5. Using potholders (skillet handle will be hot), remove skillet from oven. Transfer tenderloin to cutting board, tent loosely with aluminum foil, and let rest for 10 minutes.

6. Meanwhile, being careful of hot skillet handle, transfer glaze left in skillet to small bowl and stir in remaining 1 tablespoon maple syrup. Brush tenderloin with 1 tablespoon glaze, then slice ¼ inch thick. Serve pork, passing remaining glaze separately.

herb-rubbed pork tenderloin with fennel and artichokes

why this recipe works We wanted a simple recipe for pork tenderloin inspired by the flavors of Provence. Since the flavor of pork tenderloin is so mild, it benefits from bold seasoning, and we opted to coat ours with a dry rub. Some herbes de Provence plus a little salt and pepper hit the mark, and as a bonus its potent flavor allowed us to skip the step of browning the tenderloin before putting it in the oven. To make this a one-dish meal, we prepared a flavorful accompaniment of fennel, artichoke hearts, olives, and cherry tomatoes. Because the pork cooked quickly, we found that the fennel needed a jump start in the microwave before being added to the baking dish with the other vegetables. If the pork is enhanced (injected with a salt solution), do not brine. If brining the pork, do not season with salt in step 1. To thaw frozen artichokes quickly, microwave them, covered, for 3 to 5 minutes, drain well in a colander, and thoroughly pat dry with paper towels.

serves 2
total time: 1 hour

1 (12-ounce) pork tenderloin, trimmed and brined if desired (see page 169)

1 teaspoon herbes de Provence

Salt and pepper

1 fennel bulb, stalks discarded, bulb halved, cored, and sliced ½ inch thick

5 ounces frozen artichoke hearts, thawed and patted dry

¼ cup pitted niçoise or kalamata olives, halved

1 tablespoon extra-virgin olive oil

6 ounces cherry tomatoes, halved

1 teaspoon grated lemon zest

1 tablespoon minced fresh parsley

1. Adjust oven rack to lower-middle position and heat oven to 450 degrees. Pat tenderloin dry with paper towels, rub evenly with herbes de Provence, and season with salt and pepper.

2. Combine fennel and 1 tablespoon water in medium bowl, cover, and microwave until fennel is softened, 2 to 3 minutes. Drain fennel well, then toss with artichokes, olives, and oil and season with salt and pepper.

3. Arrange vegetables in 8-inch square baking dish. Lay tenderloin on top of vegetables and roast tenderloin until meat registers 145 degrees, 25 to 30 minutes, flipping tenderloin halfway through roasting. Transfer tenderloin to cutting board and tent loosely with aluminum foil.

4. Stir tomatoes and lemon zest into vegetables and continue to roast until fennel is tender and tomatoes have softened, about 10 minutes. Stir parsley into vegetables and season with salt and pepper to taste. Slice tenderloin ¼ inch thick and serve with vegetables.

stir-fried pork with shiitakes and snow peas

why this recipe works For a super-easy pork stir-fry that could be on the table faster than delivery or take-out, we paired quick-cooking pork tenderloin with earthy mushrooms, sweet snow peas, and crisp bean sprouts for a pleasing contrast of textures and flavors. We knew our mild pork would benefit from a bold sauce; a combination of sweet hoisin sauce, salty soy sauce, tart rice vinegar, and spicy red pepper flakes added just the right complexity with minimal ingredients. Marinating the pork in some of the sauce along with a little cornstarch ensured that it was well seasoned and stayed tender when cooked over high heat. A little ginger and garlic rounded out the flavors of this simple yet satisfying one-dish meal. To make the pork easier to slice, freeze it for 15 minutes. Serve with Simple White Rice (page 164).

serves 2
total time: 40 minutes

½ cup water

3 tablespoons vegetable oil

2 tablespoons hoisin sauce

2 tablespoons soy sauce

1 teaspoon rice vinegar

¼ teaspoon red pepper flakes

1 (12-ounce) pork tenderloin, trimmed and sliced thin

½ teaspoon cornstarch

2 garlic cloves, minced

2 teaspoons grated fresh ginger

6 ounces shiitake mushrooms, stemmed and sliced thin

4 ounces snow peas, strings removed

4 ounces (2 cups) bean sprouts

1. Whisk ¼ cup water, 1 tablespoon oil, hoisin, soy sauce, vinegar, and pepper flakes together in small bowl. Measure 1 tablespoon sauce into medium bowl, then stir in pork, cornstarch, and 1 tablespoon oil. Cover and marinate pork in refrigerator for at least 10 minutes or up to 30 minutes. Meanwhile, in separate bowl, combine garlic, ginger, and remaining 1 tablespoon oil.

2. Cook mushrooms, snow peas, and remaining ¼ cup water, covered, in 12-inch nonstick skillet over high heat until water is boiling and vegetables begin to soften, about 3 minutes. Uncover and cook until water has evaporated and vegetables are crisp-tender, about 30 seconds; transfer to bowl.

3. Return now-empty skillet to high heat. Add pork, breaking up any clumps, and cook until no longer pink and liquid has evaporated, 4 to 6 minutes. Push pork to sides of skillet. Add garlic mixture to center of skillet and cook, mashing mixture into pan, until fragrant, 15 to 30 seconds. Stir garlic mixture into pork.

4. Stir in cooked vegetables and bean sprouts. Whisk sauce to recombine, then add to skillet. Cook, stirring constantly, until sauce is thickened, about 1 minute. Serve.

garlicky pork with eggplant

why this recipe works We wanted a pork and vegetable stir-fry that would come together quickly and boast a tangy, flavor-packed Southeast Asian–inspired sauce. Pork tenderloin is ideal for stir-fries—it's easy to slice thin and cooks quickly, and its mild flavor benefits from a bold sauce. Plus, one tenderloin is the perfect amount for two servings. A simple sauce of brown sugar, fish sauce, soy sauce, and lime juice hit all the right flavor notes, and it also doubled as a marinade for the pork. Eggplant and onion provided heft and textural interest to our stir-fry, while a generous dose of garlic and black pepper provided a final punch of flavor. To make the pork easier to slice, freeze it for 15 minutes. Do not peel the eggplant, as the skin helps hold it together during cooking. Serve with Simple White Rice (page 164).

serves 2
total time: 45 minutes

¼ cup chicken broth

3 tablespoons vegetable oil

1 tablespoon packed light brown sugar

2 teaspoons fish sauce

2 teaspoons soy sauce

1 teaspoon lime juice

1 (12-ounce) pork tenderloin, trimmed and sliced thin

½ teaspoon cornstarch

6 garlic cloves, minced

½ teaspoon pepper

½ eggplant (8 ounces), cut into ¾-inch pieces

1 small onion, halved and sliced ¼ inch thick

2 tablespoons coarsely chopped fresh cilantro

1. Whisk broth, 1 tablespoon oil, sugar, fish sauce, soy sauce, and lime juice together in small bowl. Measure 1 tablespoon sauce into medium bowl, then stir in pork, cornstarch, and 1 tablespoon oil. Cover and marinate pork in refrigerator for at least 10 minutes or up to 30 minutes. Meanwhile, in separate bowl, combine garlic, pepper, and 1 teaspoon oil.

2. Heat remaining 2 teaspoons oil in 12-inch nonstick skillet over high heat until just smoking. Add eggplant and onion, cover, and cook until vegetables are softened and lightly browned, about 3 minutes. Uncover and continue to cook until vegetables are tender, about 5 minutes; transfer to bowl.

3. Return now-empty skillet to high heat. Add pork, breaking up any clumps, and cook until no longer pink and liquid has evaporated, 4 to 6 minutes. Push pork to sides of skillet. Add garlic mixture to center and cook, mashing mixture into pan, until fragrant, about 1 minute. Stir garlic mixture into pork.

4. Stir in cooked vegetables. Whisk sauce to recombine, then add to skillet. Cook, stirring constantly, until sauce is thickened, about 1 minute. Transfer to serving platter, sprinkle with cilantro, and serve.

skillet pork lo mein

why this recipe works At its best, pork lo mein features an enticing contrast of textures and flavors—springy noodles; tender, smoky pork; and a combination of crisp and tender vegetables. Meaty, flavorful country-style ribs were an ideal small-scale stand-in for the usual large cut of pork. Since we wanted our lo mein to be a one-skillet affair, we opted for dried linguine over fresh Chinese noodles, which require a large amount of water to cook properly. Napa cabbage, scallions, and shiitake mushrooms provided crunch, color, and heft, and a mixture of sesame oil and soy, oyster, and hoisin sauces provided plenty of umami flavor. When adding the pasta in step 4, stir gently to avoid breaking the noodles; after a minute or two they will soften enough to be stirred more easily. To make the pork easier to slice, freeze it for 15 minutes.

serves 2
total time: 1 hour 15 minutes

5 teaspoons soy sauce, plus extra for seasoning

1 tablespoon oyster sauce

1 tablespoon hoisin sauce

1 teaspoon toasted sesame oil

8 ounces boneless country-style pork ribs, trimmed and sliced thin crosswise

5 teaspoons vegetable oil

2 tablespoons Chinese rice wine or dry sherry

4 ounces shiitake mushrooms, stemmed, halved if large

4 scallions, white parts sliced thin, green parts cut into 1-inch pieces

1 garlic clove, minced

1 teaspoon grated fresh ginger

2½ cups water

6 ounces dried linguine

½ small head napa cabbage, cored and shredded (4 cups)

1 teaspoon Asian chili-garlic sauce

1. Whisk soy sauce, oyster sauce, hoisin, and sesame oil together in medium bowl. Measure 1 tablespoon soy sauce mixture into separate bowl; set aside. Stir pork into remaining soy sauce mixture. Cover and refrigerate pork for at least 15 minutes or up to 1 hour.

2. Heat 2 teaspoons vegetable oil in 12-inch nonstick skillet over high heat until just smoking. Add pork, breaking up any clumps, and cook, without stirring, until beginning to brown, about 1 minute. Stir pork and continue to cook until nearly cooked through, 1 to 2 minutes longer. Stir in wine and cook until almost completely evaporated, about 1 minute; transfer to clean bowl.

3. Add remaining 1 tablespoon vegetable oil to now-empty skillet and heat over high heat until just smoking. Add mushrooms and cook until light golden brown, about 5 minutes.

4. Stir in scallion whites, garlic, and ginger and cook until fragrant, about 30 seconds. Stir in water and pasta, bring to vigorous simmer, and cook, stirring often, until pasta is tender, 12 to 16 minutes. Stir in cabbage and continue to cook until cabbage is wilted and sauce is thickened, about 2 minutes longer.

5. Reduce heat to low and stir in reserved soy sauce mixture, pork, scallion greens, and chili-garlic sauce. Cook, tossing pasta gently, until well coated with sauce, about 2 minutes. Season with soy sauce to taste. Serve.

pork tacos with mango salsa

why this recipe works We wanted to capture the flavor of tacos al pastor—with their filling of slow-cooked chile-rubbed pork, chopped onion, fresh cilantro, and lime—in a weeknight recipe. Pork shoulder is the traditional cut of choice for this dish, but it was clearly out of the question for just two servings, so instead we aimed to infuse quick-cooking ground pork with smoky flavor. Chipotle chiles were exactly what we needed; they provided slow-smoked flavor and a subtle, lingering heat. A generous dose of cilantro and lime juice gave our dish an authentic flavor profile. A little shredded Monterey Jack cheese melted into the pork created a cohesive filling. Spooned into warm corn tortillas and topped with a bright mango salsa, this was a dish we could easily enjoy any night of the week. We prefer fresh mangos here, but you can substitute 1½ cups frozen mango. If your mango is unripe, add sugar as needed in step 1.

serves 2
total time: 30 minutes

1 pound mangos, peeled, pitted, and cut into ¼-inch pieces

¼ cup minced fresh cilantro

1 shallot, minced

4 teaspoons lime juice

Salt and pepper

2 teaspoons vegetable oil

1 teaspoon minced canned chipotle chile in adobo sauce

12 ounces ground pork

1 ounce Monterey Jack cheese, shredded (¼ cup)

6 (6-inch) corn tortillas, warmed

Lime wedges

1. Combine mangos, 2 tablespoons cilantro, half of shallot, 2 teaspoons lime juice, ⅛ teaspoon salt, and ⅛ teaspoon pepper in bowl; set aside.

2. Heat oil in 10-inch skillet over medium heat until shimmering. Add remaining shallot, chipotle, and ¼ teaspoon salt and cook until shallot is softened, about 2 minutes. Add pork and cook, breaking up meat with wooden spoon, until pork is no longer pink, about 5 minutes.

3. Off heat, stir in remaining 2 tablespoons cilantro, remaining 2 teaspoons lime juice, and Monterey Jack and season with salt and pepper to taste. Serve pork with warm tortillas, mango salsa, and lime wedges.

french-style white bean stew

why this recipe works Cassoulet, the French country stew celebrated for its hearty, thick-enough-to-stand-a-spoon-in texture, is a cold-weather favorite in America as well. The dish is typically made with white beans, lots of garlic and other aromatic vegetables, and an endless roster of meats including garlic sausage, duck confit, pork shoulder, and sometimes game. But you have to block off the better part of a week to make it, and then you need to invite over every neighbor to eat it. We wanted a full-flavored, cassoulet-inspired dish for two that was easy enough to put together for a weeknight dinner. Meaty chicken thighs and garlicky bratwurst were simple substitutions for duck confit and hard-to-find French sausages, and browning them created plenty of flavorful fond. Diced tomatoes and a handful of aromatics came next, along with a combination of chicken broth and dry vermouth for balanced flavor. While tradition calls for dried white beans that have been soaked overnight, we opted for canned cannellini beans, which streamlined the recipe but still offered great creamy texture and rich flavor. Torn bread, toasted in the pan before we built our stew and then sprinkled on at the end, gave the dish a classic finish and nice textural contrast. Canned navy or great Northern beans can be substituted for the cannellini beans. Traditional cassoulet uses Toulouse sausage, a garlicky sausage from France; use it if you can find it.

serves 2
total time: 1 hour 15 minutes

2½ tablespoons extra-virgin olive oil

2 slices hearty white sandwich bread, torn into ½-inch pieces

Salt and pepper

2 (5- to 7-ounce) bone-in chicken thighs, trimmed

8 ounces bratwurst or garlic sausage

1 onion, chopped fine

½ cup canned diced tomatoes, drained

3 garlic cloves, minced

1 tablespoon minced fresh thyme

1 cup chicken broth

½ cup dry vermouth or dry white wine

1 (15-ounce) can cannellini beans, rinsed

2 tablespoons minced fresh parsley

1. Heat 1½ tablespoons oil in 10-inch skillet over medium heat until shimmering. Add bread and ¼ teaspoon salt and toast, stirring frequently, until golden and crispy, 5 to 7 minutes. Transfer to bowl and set aside.

2. Pat chicken dry with paper towels and season with salt and pepper. Heat remaining 1 tablespoon oil in now-empty skillet over medium-high heat until just smoking. Add chicken, skin side down, and sausage and cook, rotating sausage occasionally but leaving chicken undisturbed, until well browned, about 5 minutes. Transfer to plate.

3. Add onion, tomatoes, and ¼ teaspoon salt to now-empty skillet and cook, stirring occasionally, until softened and beginning to brown, 5 to 7 minutes. Stir in

garlic and thyme and cook until fragrant, about 30 seconds. Stir in broth and vermouth, scraping up any browned bits. Add beans and stir to combine.

4. Add chicken, skin side up; sausage; and accumulated juices to bean mixture and bring to boil over high heat. Reduce heat to low, cover, and simmer until chicken registers 175 degrees, 10 to 15 minutes.

5. Remove lid, increase heat to medium-low, and continue to simmer until sauce is slightly thickened and liquid falls just below surface of beans, about 10 minutes longer. (Mixture will still be very loose but will continue to thicken as it sits.) Off heat, top stew with toasted bread and sprinkle with parsley. Let rest for 10 minutes before serving.

mediterranean-style fish stew

why this recipe works Since fish is naturally quick cooking, we thought a Mediterranean-inspired fish stew would make an easy yet elegant weeknight meal for two. To build an intensely flavorful base in a short amount of time, we sautéed a generous amount of onion and fennel in fruity extra-virgin olive oil. A few ounces of smoky chorizo sausage contributed hearty flavor and spicy complexity to the stew. White wine, diced tomatoes, and a bottle of clam juice gave the broth brightness, a welcome acidity, and just the right amount of brininess. We chose quick-cooking, tender cod and cut the fillets into substantial pieces that wouldn't fall apart. Just a few minutes of simmering in our flavor-packed broth was enough to cook the fish through. Serve with crusty bread or Simple White Rice (page 164).

serves 2
total time: 45 minutes

1 tablespoon extra-virgin olive oil, plus extra for serving

4 ounces chorizo sausage, cut into ½-inch pieces

1 small onion, chopped fine

½ fennel bulb, stalks discarded, bulb cored and sliced thin

2 garlic cloves, minced

⅓ cup dry white wine

1 (14.5-ounce) can diced tomatoes

1 (8-ounce) bottle clam juice

12 ounces skinless cod fillets, 1 to 1½ inches thick, cut into 2-inch pieces

Salt and pepper

1 tablespoon minced fresh parsley

1. Heat oil in medium saucepan over medium heat until shimmering. Add chorizo, onion, and fennel and cook until vegetables are softened, about 8 minutes. Stir in garlic and cook until fragrant, about 30 seconds. Stir in wine, scraping up any browned bits. Stir in tomatoes with their juice and clam juice, bring to simmer, and cook until flavors meld, about 10 minutes.

2. Season cod with salt and pepper. Nestle cod into stew mixture, spoon some sauce over fillets, and bring to simmer. Reduce heat to medium-low, cover, and simmer until cod flakes apart when gently prodded with paring knife and registers 140 degrees, about 5 minutes. Gently stir in parsley and season with salt and pepper to taste. Drizzle individual portions with extra oil before serving.

lemon-herb cod with crispy garlic potatoes

why this recipe works When cooking for two, we wanted to keep clean up as simple as possible by developing an easy one-dish dinner of flaky cod and crispy roasted potatoes. For potatoes that would cook through quickly, we sliced russet potatoes thin, tossed them with oil and garlic, and shingled them into two piles in a greased baking dish. We roasted the potatoes until they were spotty brown and tender, then added the cod fillets—topped with pieces of butter, sprigs of thyme, and slices of lemon—and slid it all back into the oven. After just 15 more minutes, we had a perfect dinner of moist, subtly flavored cod and crispy, garlicky potatoes. Try to purchase cod fillets that are similar in size so that they cook at the same rate. If the fillets are much thinner than 1 inch, simply fold them over to make them thicker. Halibut and haddock are good substitutes for the cod.

serves 2
total time: 1 hour

2 tablespoons extra-virgin olive oil

2 (8-ounce) russet potatoes, unpeeled, sliced ¼ inch thick (about 18 slices)

2 garlic cloves, minced

Salt and pepper

2 (6- to 8-ounce) skinless cod fillets, 1 to 1½ inches thick

1 tablespoon unsalted butter, cut into ¼-inch pieces

2 sprigs fresh thyme

½ lemon, sliced thin

1. Adjust oven rack to lower-middle position and heat oven to 425 degrees. Brush 13 by 9-inch baking dish with 1 tablespoon oil.

2. Toss potatoes with remaining 1 tablespoon oil and garlic and season with salt and pepper. Shingle potatoes into baking dish in 2 rectangular piles measuring 4 by 6 inches. Roast potatoes until spotty brown and just tender, 30 to 35 minutes, rotating dish halfway through roasting.

3. Pat cod dry with paper towels and season with salt and pepper. Carefully place 1 fillet, skinned side down, on top of each potato pile. Top fillets with butter pieces, thyme sprigs, and lemon slices. Roast cod and potatoes until fish flakes apart when gently prodded with paring knife and registers 140 degrees, about 15 minutes.

4. Slide spatula underneath potatoes and fillets and gently transfer to individual plates. Serve.

braised halibut with leeks and mustard

why this recipe works When it comes to methods for cooking fish, braising is often overlooked. But this approach, which requires cooking the fish in a small amount of liquid so that it gently simmers and steams, has a lot going for it: The moist heat provides a gentle—and thus forgiving—cooking environment, all but guaranteeing succulent fish. Plus, braised fish can easily become a one-pot meal; the cooking liquid becomes a sauce, and it's easy to add vegetables to the pan to cook at the same time. We chose halibut for its sweet, delicate flavor and firm texture, which made for easier handling. Because the portion of the fillets submerged in liquid cooked more quickly than the upper half that cooked as a result of steaming, we cooked the fillets for a few minutes in the pan on just one side and then braised the fillets parcooked side up so that both sides reached doneness at the same time. Leeks made an ideal accompaniment: They held their shape, cooked through quickly, and added subtle flavor to the mild white fish. For the cooking liquid, wine supplemented by the juices released by the fish and leeks during cooking delivered a sauce with balanced flavor and just the right amount of brightness. Butter added some much-needed richness and a velvety texture. We prefer to prepare this recipe with halibut, but a similar firm-fleshed white fish such as striped bass or sea bass that is between ¾ and 1 inch thick can be substituted. To ensure that your fish cooks evenly, purchase fillets that are similarly shaped and uniformly thick.

serves 2
total time: 30 minutes

2 (6- to 8-ounce) skinless halibut fillets, ¾ to 1 inch thick

Salt and pepper

3 tablespoons unsalted butter

1 medium leek, white and light green parts only, halved lengthwise, sliced thin, and washed thoroughly

½ teaspoon Dijon mustard

⅓ cup dry white wine

½ teaspoon lemon juice, plus lemon wedges for serving

½ tablespoon minced fresh parsley

1. Sprinkle halibut fillets with ¼ teaspoon salt. Melt butter in 8-inch skillet over low heat. Place halibut in skillet, skinned side up, increase heat to medium, and cook, shaking pan occasionally, until butter begins to brown (halibut should not brown), 2 to 3 minutes. Using spatula, carefully transfer halibut to large plate, raw side down.

2. Add leeks, mustard, and ¼ teaspoon salt to skillet and cook, stirring frequently, until leeks begin to soften, 1 to 2 minutes. Add wine and bring to gentle simmer. Place halibut, raw side down, on top of leeks. Cover skillet and cook, adjusting heat to maintain gentle simmer, until halibut registers 135 to 140 degrees, 10 to 14 minutes. Remove skillet from heat and, using 2 spatulas, transfer halibut and leeks to serving platter or individual plates. Tent loosely with aluminum foil.

3. Return skillet to high heat and cook until sauce is thickened, 30 to 60 seconds. Remove pan from heat, stir in lemon juice, and season with salt and pepper to taste. Spoon sauce over halibut and sprinkle with parsley. Serve immediately with lemon wedges.

thai-style fish and creamy coconut rice packets

why this recipe works Cooking fish *en papillote*, or in a packet, is ideal when cooking for two. Not only do the fillets cook evenly, but the technique encourages the fish to absorb all the flavors within the packet, and clean up is a breeze. For a Thai-inspired take on this dish, we combined meaty halibut fillets and rice with a quick yet potent sauce made from coconut milk, green curry paste, lime zest, and a little cilantro, which we simply whisked together. The sauce did more than infuse the fish with flavor; it also provided a burst of color and transformed the rice into a rich, creamy accompaniment for the halibut. A sprinkle of cilantro and a squeeze of lime just before serving highlighted the flavor of the sauce and brightened the dish. Try to purchase halibut fillets that are similar in size so that they cook at the same rate. If the fillets are much thinner than ¾ inch, simply fold them over to make them thicker. Cod and haddock are good substitutes for the halibut. You can use fresh rice, leftover rice, or store-bought precooked rice here (see Simple White Rice, page 164).

serves 2
total time: 40 minutes

½ cup canned coconut milk

¼ cup minced fresh cilantro

4 teaspoons Thai green curry paste

1 teaspoon grated lime zest, plus lime wedges

2 (6- to 8-ounce) skinless halibut fillets, ¾ to 1 inch thick

Salt and pepper

2 cups cooked rice

Lime wedges

1. Adjust oven rack to middle position and heat oven to 400 degrees. Whisk coconut milk, 3 tablespoons cilantro, curry paste, and lime zest together in bowl.

2. Pat halibut dry with paper towels and season with salt and pepper. Cut two 14 by 12-inch rectangles of aluminum foil and lay them flat on counter. Mound 1 cup cooked rice in center of each piece of foil, then place fillets on top. Spoon coconut mixture over top of fillets, then tightly crimp foil into packets.

3. Set packets on rimmed baking sheet and bake until halibut flakes apart when gently prodded with paring knife and registers 140 degrees, 18 to 20 minutes. (To check temperature, poke thermometer through foil of one packet and into halibut.) Carefully open packets, allowing steam to escape away from you. Sprinkle fillets with remaining 1 tablespoon cilantro and serve with lime wedges.

preparing fish and rice packets

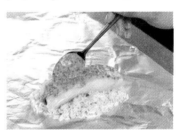

1. Lay two 14 by 12-inch lengths of aluminum foil flat on counter and pile 1 cup of rice in center of each. Lay 1 fish fillet on top of rice; spoon sauce over fish.

2. Fold foil over fish and rice to make packets, then fold edges together tightly to seal.

chili-glazed salmon with bok choy

why this recipe works To turn glazed salmon into a simple one-dish meal, we needed to find a way to prepare perfectly cooked fish with a crisp, well-browned crust alongside an easy vegetable side all in the same skillet. Using a nonstick skillet ensured that the browned crust stayed on the fish, not stuck to the pan. Some sweet chili sauce mixed with a little savory fish sauce and fresh ginger created a boldly flavored glaze that complemented the rich salmon. A pinch of cornstarch helped thicken the glaze so that it nicely coated the fish. Baby bok choy sautéed until lightly browned paired perfectly with the salmon and our Asian-inspired glaze. Try to purchase center-cut salmon fillets of similar size so that they cook at the same rate. Be sure to use sweet chili sauce here; hot chili sauce (such as chili-garlic sauce) will make the glaze too spicy and thin. If you purchase skin-on fillets, follow the instructions below to remove the skin.

serves 2
total time: 30 minutes

2 tablespoons Asian sweet chili sauce

1 tablespoon fish sauce

1½ teaspoons grated fresh ginger

¼ teaspoon cornstarch

2 tablespoons vegetable oil

2 heads baby bok choy (4 ounces each), halved

2 (6- to 8-ounce) skinless salmon fillets, 1 to 1½ inches thick

Salt and pepper

Lime wedges

1. Whisk chili sauce, fish sauce, ginger, and cornstarch together in small bowl. Heat 1 tablespoon oil in 10-inch nonstick skillet over high heat until shimmering. Add bok choy, cut side down, to skillet and cook until lightly browned on both sides, 1 to 2 minutes per side; transfer to plate.

2. Pat salmon dry with paper towels and season with salt and pepper. Heat remaining 1 tablespoon oil in now-empty skillet over medium-high heat until just smoking. Lay fillets in skillet and cook until browned on first side, about 5 minutes. Using tongs, gently flip fillets and continue to cook until center of salmon is still translucent when checked with tip of paring knife and registers 125 degrees (for medium-rare), 3 to 5 minutes. Holding fillets in place with spatula, carefully pour off any rendered fat in skillet. Off heat, add chili sauce mixture to skillet with salmon and gently flip fillets once or twice to coat. Transfer fillets to serving platter.

3. Add bok choy to skillet with glaze and toss until coated; transfer to platter with salmon. Serve with lime wedges.

skinning salmon fillets

1. Using tip of boning knife (or sharp chef's knife), begin to cut skin away from fish at corner of fillet.

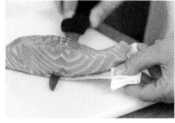

2. When enough skin is exposed, grasp it firmly with piece of paper towel, hold it taut, and carefully slice rest of skin off flesh.

miso-marinated salmon

why this recipe works Miso-glazed salmon promises firm, flavorful fish with a glazed, lacquer-like exterior, but it typically takes 3 days to prepare—too much of a time commitment when cooking for just two. We hoped to shorten the process without sacrificing this dish's characteristic depth of flavor and luxurious texture. We found that we could simply reduce the marinade time to between 6 and 24 hours and still achieve the complex, sweet-savory flavor, silky interior, and contrasting crispy exterior that this dish is known for. A marinade composed of miso, sugar, mirin, and sake allowed for flavor penetration, moisture retention, and good browning by drying the fish's surface. Broiling the fish at a safe distance from the heating element ensured a caramelized exterior without risk of overcooking the flesh. Note that the salmon needs to marinate for at least 6 or up to 24 hours before cooking. Yellow, red, or brown rice miso can be used instead of white. If the edges of the salmon begin to get too brown, you may need to shield them with aluminum foil in step 3.

serves 2
total time: 30 minutes
(plus 6 hours for marinating)

¼ cup white miso paste

2 tablespoons sugar

1½ tablespoons sake

1½ tablespoons mirin

2 (6- to 8-ounce) skin-on salmon fillets, 1 to 1½ inches thick

1 tablespoon minced fresh parsley

Lemon wedges

1. Whisk miso, sugar, sake, and mirin together in medium bowl until sugar and miso are dissolved (mixture will be thick). Dip each fillet into miso mixture to evenly coat all flesh sides. Place salmon, skin side down, in baking dish and pour any remaining miso mixture over fillets. Cover with plastic wrap and refrigerate for at least 6 hours or up to 24 hours.

2. Adjust oven rack 8 inches from broiler element and heat broiler. Place wire rack in rimmed baking sheet and cover with aluminum foil. Using your fingers, scrape miso mixture from fillets (do not rinse) and place salmon, skin side down, on foil, leaving 1 inch between fillets.

3. Broil salmon until deeply browned and center of fish is still translucent when checked with tip of paring knife and registers 125 degrees (for medium-rare), 8 to 12 minutes, rotating sheet halfway through cooking. Transfer to platter, sprinkle with parsley, and serve with lemon wedges.

crispy salmon cakes with sweet and tangy tartar sauce

why this recipe works We love classic, elegant salmon fillets for dinner, but we were looking for a different way to incorporate this rich, versatile fish into our cooking for two repertoire. Individual cakes seemed like a great option, as one 10-ounce fillet yielded a perfectly sized batch of cakes for two. We wanted to use just a few choice ingredients and minimal binders to ensure that the salmon's robust flavor took center stage. Fresh salmon easily beat out canned, and we ditched the typical potato binder in favor of mayonnaise and bread crumbs. To chop the salmon, we quickly pulsed 1-inch pieces in the food processor. This gave us both larger chunks for a substantial texture and smaller pieces that helped the cakes hold together. A coating of ultracrisp panko bread crumbs provided a good crust. Dijon mustard, shallot, lemon juice, and parsley boosted the flavor of the cakes without overwhelming the flavor of the salmon, and a quick tartar sauce completed the dish. Be sure to use raw salmon here; do not substitute cooked salmon. Do not overprocess the salmon in step 2 or the cakes will have a pasty texture. If you purchase skin-on fillets, see page 112 for information on removing the skin.

serves 2
total time: 35 minutes

tartar sauce
⅓ cup mayonnaise

1 tablespoon sweet pickle relish

1½ teaspoons capers, rinsed and minced

1 teaspoon white wine vinegar

¼ teaspoon Worcestershire sauce

Salt and pepper

salmon cakes
1 (10-ounce) skinless salmon fillet, cut into 1-inch pieces

2 tablespoons plus ½ cup panko bread crumbs

1 tablespoon minced fresh parsley

1 tablespoon mayonnaise

1 small shallot, minced

2 teaspoons lemon juice

½ teaspoon Dijon mustard

Salt and pepper

Pinch cayenne pepper

⅓ cup vegetable oil

1. for the tartar sauce Whisk all ingredients together in bowl and season with salt and pepper to taste; set aside.

2. for the salmon cakes Pulse salmon in food processor until there is an even mix of finely minced and coarsely chopped pieces of salmon, about 2 pulses, scraping down sides of bowl as needed.

3. Combine 2 tablespoons panko, parsley, mayonnaise, shallot, lemon juice, mustard, ½ teaspoon salt, ¼ teaspoon pepper, and cayenne in bowl. Gently fold in processed salmon until just combined.

4. Spread remaining ½ cup panko in shallow dish. Scrape salmon mixture onto small baking sheet. Divide mixture into 4 equal portions and gently flatten each portion into 1-inch-thick patty. Carefully coat each cake with panko, then return to sheet.

5. Line large plate with triple layer of paper towels. Heat oil in 10-inch skillet over medium-high heat until shimmering. Gently place salmon cakes in skillet and cook, without moving, until golden brown and crisp on both sides, 2 to 3 minutes per side. Drain cakes briefly on paper towel–lined plate. Serve with tartar sauce.

seared scallop salad with snap peas and radishes

why this recipe works For an elegant yet simple dinner salad, we wanted to pair tender seared sea scallops with fresh spring vegetables. Because the scallops would be the star of the dish, we needed to ensure that they were perfectly cooked. Sandwiching the scallops between dish towels and letting them drain for 10 minutes before cooking rid them of excess moisture that would prevent them from developing a well-browned crust in the skillet. After seasoning them with salt and pepper, we seared them in a hot skillet for a few minutes until their centers were just opaque and their exteriors were caramelized and flavorful. For the salad, we tossed delicate mesclun greens, fresh sugar snap peas, and thinly sliced peppery radishes with a simple vinaigrette and arranged the delicate scallops on top. We recommend buying "dry" scallops, which don't have chemical additives and taste better than "wet." Dry scallops will look ivory or pinkish; wet scallops are bright white.

serves 2
total time: 25 minutes

12 ounces large sea scallops, tendons removed

1 tablespoon red wine vinegar

½ teaspoon Dijon mustard

3 tablespoons extra-virgin olive oil

6 ounces sugar snap peas, strings removed, halved crosswise

4 ounces (4 cups) mesclun

4 radishes, trimmed and sliced thin

1 shallot, sliced thin

Salt and pepper

1. Place scallops on large plate lined with clean dish towel. Place second clean dish towel on top of scallops and press gently on towel to blot liquid. Let scallops sit at room temperature for 10 minutes while towels absorb moisture.

2. Meanwhile, combine vinegar and mustard in large bowl. Whisking constantly, drizzle 2 tablespoons oil into vinegar mixture in slow, steady stream. Add snap peas, mesclun, radishes, and shallot and gently toss to coat. Season with salt and pepper to taste. Divide salad among individual plates or transfer to serving platter.

3. Season scallops with salt and pepper. Heat remaining 1 tablespoon oil in 12-inch nonstick skillet over high heat until just smoking. Add scallops in single layer, flat side down, and cook, without moving, until well browned, 1½ to 2 minutes. Flip scallops and continue to cook until sides of scallops are firm and centers are opaque, 30 to 90 seconds (remove smaller scallops as they finish cooking). Arrange scallops over salad. Serve.

shrimp scampi

why this recipe works To achieve the perfect shrimp scampi for two, we relied on a few test kitchen tricks to ensure flavorful, well-cooked shrimp. First, we brined the shrimp in salt and sugar to season them throughout and to keep them moist and juicy. Next we poached the delicate shellfish in wine; poaching—rather than sautéing—the shrimp allowed them to cook evenly and gently. We wanted our scampi sauce to be creamy and robust with good shrimp flavor, so we started by making a stock from the shrimp shells. A generous amount of sliced garlic contributed potent but clean garlic flavor, and to keep the sauce silky and emulsified we added a teaspoon of cornstarch. Extra-large shrimp (21 to 25 per pound) can be substituted for jumbo shrimp. If you use them, reduce the cooking time in step 3 by 1 to 2 minutes. We prefer untreated shrimp, but if your shrimp are treated with sodium or preservatives like sodium tripolyphosphate, skip the brining in step 1 and add ⅛ teaspoon of salt to the sauce in step 4. Serve with crusty bread.

serves 2
total time: 50 minutes

4½ teaspoons salt

1 tablespoon sugar

12 ounces shell-on jumbo shrimp (16 to 20 per pound), peeled, deveined, and tails removed, shells reserved

4½ teaspoons extra-virgin olive oil

½ cup dry white wine

2 sprigs fresh thyme

4½ teaspoons lemon juice, plus lemon wedges for serving

½ teaspoon cornstarch

4 garlic cloves, sliced thin

¼ teaspoon red pepper flakes

⅛ teaspoon pepper

2 tablespoons unsalted butter, cut into ½-inch pieces and chilled

1½ teaspoons chopped fresh parsley

1. Dissolve salt and sugar in 2 cups cold water in container. Submerge shrimp in brine, cover, and refrigerate for 15 minutes. Remove shrimp from brine and pat dry with paper towels.

2. Heat 1½ teaspoons oil in 10-inch skillet over high heat until shimmering. Add shrimp shells and cook, stirring frequently, until they begin to turn spotty brown and skillet starts to brown, 2 to 4 minutes. Remove skillet from heat and carefully add wine and thyme sprigs. When bubbling subsides, return skillet to medium heat and simmer gently, stirring occasionally, for 4 minutes. Strain mixture through colander set over large bowl. Discard solids and reserve liquid (you should have about ⅓ cup). Wipe out skillet with paper towels.

3. Combine lemon juice and cornstarch in small bowl. Heat remaining 1 tablespoon oil, garlic, pepper flakes, and pepper in now-empty skillet over medium-low heat, stirring occasionally, until garlic is fragrant and just beginning to brown at edges, 3 to 5 minutes. Add reserved wine mixture, increase heat to high, and bring to simmer. Reduce heat to medium, add shrimp, cover, and cook, stirring occasionally, until shrimp are just opaque, 5 to 7 minutes. Remove skillet from heat and, using slotted spoon, transfer shrimp to bowl.

4. Return skillet to medium heat, add lemon juice–cornstarch mixture, and cook until slightly thickened, about 1 minute. Remove from heat and whisk in butter and parsley until combined. Return shrimp and any accumulated juices to skillet and toss to combine. Serve, passing lemon wedges separately.

campanelle with roasted garlic, shrimp, and feta

why this recipe works For a simple shrimp and pasta dish perfectly portioned for two people, we wanted to get big flavor out of a small shopping list. Rather than sautéing the garlic, we decided to roast it to bring a sweet, nutty dimension to our sauce. We found that we could speed up the roasting time if we separated and peeled the cloves before putting them in a covered baking dish with some olive oil. After 20 minutes we had soft, caramelized cloves of garlic, which we mashed with the oil to form a savory sauce. Adding the shrimp right to the garlic and oil mixture to cook through infused it with lots of flavor in a short amount of time, and a little crumbled feta added a salty tang that complemented the sweetness of the roasted garlic and shrimp. Other pasta shapes can be substituted for the campanelle; however, their cup measurements may vary.

serves 2
total time: 1 hour 10 minutes

2½ tablespoons extra-virgin olive oil

6 garlic cloves, peeled

Salt and pepper

8 ounces medium-large shrimp (31 to 40 per pound), peeled, deveined, and tails removed

6 ounces (2 cups) campanelle

1½ ounces feta cheese, crumbled (⅓ cup)

⅓ cup chopped fresh basil

1. Adjust oven rack to upper-middle position and heat oven to 425 degrees. Combine oil, garlic, ⅛ teaspoon salt, and ¼ teaspoon pepper in small baking dish and cover with aluminum foil. Bake, stirring occasionally, until garlic is caramelized and soft, about 20 minutes. Let cool slightly, then mash garlic and oil into paste with fork. Stir in shrimp and continue to bake, uncovered, until shrimp are opaque throughout, about 10 minutes.

2. Meanwhile, bring 4 quarts water to boil in large pot. Add pasta and 1 tablespoon salt and cook, stirring often, until al dente. Reserve ½ cup cooking water, then drain pasta and return it to pot. Add shrimp mixture, feta, and basil and toss to combine. Season with salt and pepper to taste, and adjust consistency with reserved cooking water as needed. Serve.

singapore noodles with shrimp

why this recipe works Singapore noodles—an almost fluffy stir-fry featuring thin rice vermicelli noodles, vegetables, and shrimp bound together with the pungent flavor of curry powder—is a dish with a devoted following. We wanted our own home-cooked version of this takeout favorite, and we wanted just enough for two without a week's worth of leftovers. Using soy sauce, mirin, and chicken broth, we whipped up a sauce that achieved an ideal salty-sweet balance. We found that soaking the noodles in hot water softened them just enough while still retaining a pleasantly tender chew. For the vegetable component, sliced shallots and red bell pepper added crunch and freshness. Seared shrimp turned our noodles into a one-dish meal. Do not substitute other types of noodles for the rice vermicelli here. You can find dried rice vermicelli in the Asian section of most supermarkets.

serves 2
total time: 35 minutes

4 ounces rice vermicelli

8 ounces extra-large shrimp (21 to 25 per pound), peeled, deveined, and tails removed

1½ teaspoons curry powder

⅛ teaspoon sugar

4 teaspoons vegetable oil

3 shallots, sliced thin

1 red bell pepper, stemmed, seeded, and cut into ¼-inch-wide strips

1 garlic clove, minced

½ cup chicken broth

3 tablespoons soy sauce

2 teaspoons mirin

½ teaspoon Sriracha sauce

2 ounces (1 cup) bean sprouts

¼ cup minced fresh cilantro

1. Cover noodles with very hot tap water in large bowl and stir to separate. Let noodles soak until softened, pliable, and limp but not fully tender, about 20 minutes; drain.

2. Meanwhile, pat shrimp dry with paper towels and toss with ¼ teaspoon curry powder and sugar. Heat 2 teaspoons oil in 12-inch nonstick skillet over medium-high heat until just smoking. Add shrimp in single layer and cook, without stirring, until beginning to brown, about 1 minute. Stir shrimp and continue to cook until spotty brown and just pink around edges, about 30 seconds longer; transfer to bowl.

3. Add remaining 2 teaspoons oil to now-empty skillet and heat over medium heat until shimmering. Add shallots, bell pepper, and remaining 1¼ teaspoons curry powder and cook until vegetables are softened, about 5 minutes. Stir in garlic and cook until fragrant, about 30 seconds.

4. Stir in broth, soy sauce, mirin, Sriracha, noodles, and shrimp and any accumulated juices and cook, tossing gently, until noodles, shrimp, and vegetables are well coated with sauce, 2 to 3 minutes. Stir in bean sprouts and cilantro and serve.

pad thai

why this recipe works Authentic recipes for pad thai have a mile-long ingredient list that features at least a few hard-to-find ingredients, so when cooking for two, we find making pad thai at home isn't always worth the effort. We wanted to develop a recipe that would be full of authentic flavor but streamlined enough that it would be easy to prepare in a small batch. Soaking flat rice noodles in just-boiled water ensured that they cooked to the proper tender yet resilient texture when added to our stir-fry. To achieve the right balance of flavors in the sauce, we used a combination of readily available supermarket ingredients: fish sauce for salty-sweet pungency, brown sugar for complex sweetness, a pinch of cayenne for subtle heat, and rice vinegar and lime juice for acidity. Sautéed shrimp, scrambled egg, chopped peanuts, bean sprouts, and scallions are essential components of pad thai and provided just the right flavors and textures. We prefer the rich molasses flavor of dark brown sugar in this recipe, but you can substitute light brown sugar in a pinch.

serves 2
total time: 40 minutes

sauce
3 tablespoons lime juice (2 limes)

3 tablespoons water

2½ tablespoons packed dark brown sugar

2 tablespoons fish sauce

1½ tablespoons vegetable oil

2 teaspoons rice vinegar

⅛ teaspoon cayenne pepper

noodles, shrimp, and toppings
4 ounces (¼-inch-wide) rice noodles

6 ounces medium shrimp (41 to 50 per pound), peeled and deveined

2 tablespoons vegetable oil

Salt

1 small shallot, minced

1 garlic clove, minced

1 large egg, lightly beaten

2 ounces (1 cup) bean sprouts

2 tablespoons chopped dry-roasted peanuts, plus extra for garnish

2 scallions, green parts only, sliced thin

2 tablespoons fresh cilantro leaves

1. for the sauce Whisk all ingredients together in bowl and set aside.

2. for the noodles, shrimp, and toppings Bring 4 quarts water to boil in large pot. Remove boiling water from heat, add rice noodles, and let stand, stirring occasionally, until noodles are just tender, about 10 minutes. Drain noodles and set aside.

3. Pat shrimp dry with paper towels. Heat 1 tablespoon oil in 10-inch nonstick skillet over medium-high heat until just smoking. Add shrimp and pinch salt and cook, stirring occasionally, until shrimp are opaque, 2 to 3 minutes; transfer shrimp to plate.

4. Heat remaining 1 tablespoon oil in now-empty skillet over medium heat until shimmering. Add shallot, garlic, and pinch salt and cook, stirring constantly, until light golden brown, about 1½ minutes. Stir in egg and cook, stirring constantly, until scrambled and barely moist, about 20 seconds.

5. Add drained rice noodles and toss to combine. Add sauce, increase heat to medium-high, and cook, tossing constantly, until noodles are evenly coated, about 1 minute.

6. Add shrimp, bean sprouts, peanuts, and half of scallions and continue to cook, tossing constantly, until noodles are tender, about 2 minutes. (If not yet tender, add 2 tablespoons water to skillet and continue to cook until tender.) Transfer noodles to platter and sprinkle with cilantro, extra peanuts, and remaining scallions. Serve.

steamed mussels in white wine with parsley

why this recipe works The French bistro classic known as *moules marinières* has just a few simple ingredients—mussels, shallot, garlic, parsley, white wine, and butter—but their combined effect is extraordinary. The mussels are tender and briny, and the rich broth is perfect for sopping up with chunks of a rustic baguette. To make our own scaled-down version for a party of two, we started by sautéing a shallot and a couple of cloves of minced garlic in butter. We then added some white wine and a bay leaf and brought everything to a simmer, which allowed the flavors of our broth a chance to meld. Finally, we nestled in the mussels to gently steam. Once the mussels opened, we removed them and enriched the broth with a pat of butter and a bit of heavy cream. A sprinkling of fresh parsley finished this remarkably easy dish with a touch of color and freshness. Any type of mussel will work here; if you can't find mussels or prefer clams, littleneck or cherry-stone clams can also be substituted (large clams will require 9 to 10 minutes of steaming time). Serve this dish with crusty bread or garlic toasts.

serves 2
total time: 30 minutes

2 tablespoons unsalted butter

1 shallot, minced

2 garlic cloves, minced

⅔ cup dry white wine

1 bay leaf

2 pounds mussels, scrubbed and debearded

2 tablespoons heavy cream

3 tablespoons minced fresh parsley

Salt and pepper

1. Melt 1 tablespoon butter in Dutch oven over medium heat. Add shallot and cook until softened, about 2 minutes. Stir in garlic and cook until fragrant, about 30 seconds. Stir in wine and bay leaf, bring to simmer, and cook until flavors meld, about 2 minutes.

2. Increase heat to high and add mussels. Cover and cook, stirring occasionally, until mussels open, 3 to 7 minutes.

3. Using slotted spoon, transfer opened mussels to large serving bowl, leaving cooking liquid in pot. Discard bay leaf and any mussels that have not opened.

4. Stir cream and remaining 1 tablespoon butter into cooking liquid, bring to simmer, and cook until butter is melted and liquid is slightly thickened, about 1 minute. Off heat, stir in parsley and season with salt and pepper to taste. Pour sauce over mussels and serve immediately.

variations

steamed mussels in coconut milk with cilantro
Add 1 sliced jalapeño chile to pot with shallot. Substitute ¾ cup canned coconut milk for wine and cilantro for parsley. Stir in 1 teaspoon lime juice, 1 teaspoon packed brown sugar, and 1 teaspoon fish sauce with cilantro in step 4.

steamed mussels in white wine with tomato and basil
Substitute chopped fresh basil for parsley. Add 1 finely chopped tomato with basil in step 4.

clams with israeli couscous, kielbasa, and fennel

why this recipe works Clams make an ideal dinner for two: You can buy just the amount you need, they're quick-cooking, and they make for an elegant meal. Littlenecks were a great starting point; to offset their brininess and give the dish more heft, we added chunks of kielbasa, which contributed big, bold flavor. White wine served as the perfect base for a potent broth in which the clams could steam, and a pat of butter contributed ample richness to counter the bright notes of the wine and clams. To make this dish a well-rounded meal, we added juicy cherry tomatoes, fennel, and couscous. Using large-grain Israeli couscous instead of the more traditional small-grain Moroccan couscous gave our dish great texture and visual appeal while providing a sturdy base for the clams and vegetables. To cook the couscous, we simply simmered it like pasta and drained it; once the clams had opened, we tossed the couscous into the broth so that it could absorb the complex flavors. Small quahogs or cherrystones are good alternatives to the littleneck clams. Be sure to use Israeli couscous in this dish; regular (or fine) couscous won't work here.

serves 2
total time: 40 minutes

1 cup Israeli couscous

1 tablespoon unsalted butter

1 small onion, chopped coarse

1 small fennel bulb (8 ounces), stalks discarded, bulb halved, cored, and chopped coarse

4 ounces kielbasa sausage, halved lengthwise and sliced ½ inch thick

1 garlic clove, minced

¼ cup dry white wine or dry vermouth

1½ pounds littleneck clams, scrubbed

6 ounces cherry tomatoes, quartered

¼ cup coarsely chopped fresh parsley

Salt and pepper

1. Bring 2 quarts water to boil in medium saucepan. Add couscous and cook, stirring often, until al dente; drain well and set aside.

2. Meanwhile, melt butter in large saucepan over medium heat. Add onion, fennel, and kielbasa and cook until vegetables are softened, about 5 minutes.

3. Stir in garlic and cook until fragrant, about 30 seconds. Stir in wine, scraping up any browned bits, and cook until slightly reduced, about 30 seconds. Stir in clams, cover, and cook, stirring occasionally, until clams open, 8 to 10 minutes.

4. Using slotted spoon, transfer opened clams to large bowl; discard any clams that have not opened.

5. Stir tomatoes, parsley, and couscous into cooking liquid left in saucepan and season with salt and pepper to taste. Portion couscous mixture into individual bowls, top with clams, and serve.

penne arrabbiata

why this recipe works To deliver an *arrabbiata* with complex flavor and not just searing heat, we looked beyond the traditional red pepper flakes and crafted a recipe that included three different types of pepper. By supplementing the pepper flakes with paprika and pickled *pepperoncini*, we built deep flavor while keeping the spiciness in check. Pecorino Romano, tomato paste, and anchovies, while difficult to detect in the sauce, added umami notes and richness to this traditionally simple sauce. Finally, using processed canned tomatoes helped bring the sauce to the table quickly and also meant we could enjoy it year-round. This recipe will work with other short tubular pastas such as ziti or rigatoni.

serves 2
total time: 50 minutes

1 (14.5-ounce) can whole peeled tomatoes

2 tablespoons extra-virgin olive oil

2 tablespoons stemmed, patted dry, and minced pepperoncini

1 tablespoon tomato paste

½ teaspoon minced garlic

½ teaspoon red pepper flakes

2 anchovy fillets, rinsed, patted dry, and minced to paste

¼ teaspoon paprika

Salt and pepper

2 tablespoons grated Pecorino Romano, plus extra for serving

6 ounces (2 cups) penne

1. Pulse tomatoes and their juice in food processor until finely chopped, about 10 pulses.

2. Heat oil, pepperoncini, tomato paste, garlic, pepper flakes, anchovies, paprika, ¼ teaspoon salt, and ¼ teaspoon pepper in medium saucepan over medium-low heat, stirring occasionally, until deep red, 7 to 8 minutes.

3. Add tomatoes and Pecorino and bring to simmer. Cook, stirring occasionally, until thickened, about 15 minutes.

4. Meanwhile, bring 4 quarts water to boil in large pot. Add pasta and 1 tablespoon salt and cook, stirring often, until al dente. Reserve ½ cup cooking water, then drain pasta and return it to pot. Add sauce and toss to combine, adjusting consistency with reserved cooking water as needed. Season with salt and pepper to taste. Serve, passing extra Pecorino separately.

risotto primavera

why this recipe works Most risotto recipes require constant stirring from start to finish, but with just two to feed, we weren't willing to spend all that time stuck by the stove. To streamline the process, we tried cooking the risotto hands-off until it was partially tender, then stirring constantly while it finished cooking. We found that just 6 minutes of stirring at the end was enough to release the necessary starch to give us remarkably creamy risotto. To make our risotto a meal, we added vegetables inspired by pasta primavera: asparagus, mushrooms, onion, and peas. Sautéing the mushrooms and onion in the pan before adding the rice deepened their flavor. Lemon juice and fresh basil brightened the dish, and Parmesan and butter added richness before serving. White, shiitake, or portobello (caps only) mushrooms can be substituted for the cremini in this recipe. High-quality Parmesan makes a big difference here.

serves 2
total time: 50 minutes

1¾ cups vegetable broth

½ cup water

4 teaspoons extra-virgin olive oil

3 ounces cremini mushrooms, trimmed and sliced thin

Salt and pepper

1 small onion, chopped fine

½ cup Arborio rice

3 ounces asparagus, trimmed and cut into ½-inch pieces

¼ cup frozen peas

¼ cup grated Parmesan cheese, plus extra for serving

2 tablespoons chopped fresh basil

1 tablespoon unsalted butter

2 teaspoons lemon juice

1. Bring broth and water to simmer in small saucepan over medium heat. Remove from heat, cover, and keep warm.

2. Heat 2 teaspoons oil in medium saucepan over medium heat until shimmering. Add mushrooms and ¼ teaspoon salt and cook, covered, until just starting to brown, about 4 minutes; transfer to bowl. Return now-empty saucepan to medium heat, add remaining 2 teaspoons oil, and heat until shimmering. Add onion and ¼ teaspoon salt and cook until just beginning to soften, about 2 minutes. Add rice and cook, stirring constantly, until grains are translucent around edges, about 1 minute.

3. Stir in 1½ cups warm broth, reduce heat to medium-low, cover, and simmer until almost all liquid is absorbed, about 12 minutes. Stir in asparagus, cover, and cook for 2 minutes. Add ½ cup broth and cook, stirring constantly, until broth is absorbed, about 3 minutes. Add remaining ¼ cup broth and peas and cook, stirring constantly, until rice is creamy and al dente, about 3 minutes.

4. Off heat, stir in cooked mushrooms, cover, and let sit until heated through, about 2 minutes. Stir in Parmesan, basil, butter, and lemon juice. Season with salt and pepper to taste. Serve, passing extra Parmesan separately.

penne with red pepper pesto (pesto calabrese)

why this recipe works Pesto calabrese trades the familiar basil–pine nut base of the Genovese style for a red pepper pesto consisting of ricotta, Parmesan, and a combination of sweet and hot peppers. For complex flavor, we used both sautéed red bell pepper—which we started covered to soften and then uncovered to develop flavorful browning—and raw red bell pepper, for fresh, fruity bite. For a little heat, we substituted dried red pepper flakes for the hard-to-find Calabrian chiles. We also added fresh tomato, onion, garlic, and basil to the pepper mixture for further complexity. A modest amount of cheese—a 2:1 ratio of ricotta to grated Parmesan—added richness, creamy body, and a salty tang without dulling the vegetables' flavor. Other short, tubular pastas can be substituted for the penne. Adjust the amount of red pepper flakes depending on how spicy you want the dish.

serves 2
total time: 1 hour

1½ red bell peppers, stemmed, seeded, and cut into ¼-inch-wide strips (2½ cups)

1½ tablespoons extra-virgin olive oil

Salt and pepper

½ small onion, chopped

1 plum tomato, cored, seeded, and chopped

¼ cup chopped fresh basil

¼–½ teaspoon red pepper flakes

½ teaspoon minced garlic

¼ cup whole-milk ricotta cheese

2 tablespoons grated Parmesan cheese, plus extra for serving

½ teaspoon white wine vinegar

8 ounces (2½ cups) penne

1. Toss two-thirds of bell peppers with 1½ teaspoons oil and ⅛ teaspoon salt in 10-inch nonstick skillet. Cover and place over medium-low heat. Cook, stirring occasionally, until bell peppers are softened and just starting to brown, about 15 minutes.

2. Add onion, tomato, basil, pepper flakes, and ¼ teaspoon garlic and continue to cook, uncovered, stirring occasionally, until onion is softened and bell peppers are browned in spots, 6 to 7 minutes longer. Remove skillet from heat and let cool for 5 minutes.

3. Place ricotta, Parmesan, remaining one-third of bell peppers, remaining ¼ teaspoon garlic, ¼ teaspoon salt, and ⅛ teaspoon pepper in bowl of food processor. Add cooked bell pepper mixture and process for 20 seconds. Scrape down sides of bowl. With processor running, add vinegar and remaining 1 tablespoon oil; process for about 20 seconds. Scrape down sides of bowl, then continue to process until smooth, about 20 seconds longer.

4. Meanwhile, bring 4 quarts water to boil in large pot. Add pasta and 1 tablespoon salt and cook, stirring often, until al dente. Reserve ½ cup cooking water, then drain pasta and return it to pot. Add pesto and toss to combine, adjusting consistency with reserved cooking water as needed. Season with salt and pepper to taste. Serve, passing extra Parmesan separately.

garlicky spaghetti with lemon and pine nuts

why this recipe works We found that the key to a simple but flavor-packed spaghetti made from pantry ingredients is using plenty of garlic—and making the most of it. Mincing the garlic encouraged it to cook evenly. We toasted the garlic over low heat in extra-virgin olive oil until it cooked to a pale golden brown; any darker and its delicate, buttery sweetness became bitter and harsh. We cooked our spaghetti in just 1 quart of salted water to ensure that the pasta cooking liquid would be loaded with starch. Reserving a portion of this liquid and adding it to the cooked spaghetti helped the garlic-oil mixture cling to the pasta and gave the dish a perfect—not greasy—texture. Adding raw minced garlic near the end of cooking added a subtle kick that balanced the toasted garlic's sweetness. Fresh basil provided a brightness just before serving, while pine nuts offered some richness and crunch. A garlic press makes quick work of uniformly mincing the garlic, which in turn ensures that the garlic browns evenly. Serve with a Basic Green Salad (page 169) for a light, quick supper.

serves 2
total time: 40 minutes

2 tablespoons extra-virgin olive oil

1 tablespoon plus ¼ teaspoon minced garlic

⅛ teaspoon red pepper flakes

8 ounces spaghetti

Salt and pepper

1 teaspoon grated lemon zest plus 1 tablespoon juice

½ cup chopped fresh basil

¼ cup grated Parmesan cheese, plus extra for serving

¼ cup pine nuts, toasted

1. Combine oil and 1 tablespoon garlic in 8-inch nonstick skillet. Cook over low heat, stirring occasionally, until garlic is pale golden brown, 5 to 7 minutes. Off heat, stir in pepper flakes; set aside.

2. Bring 1 quart water to boil in large saucepan. Add pasta and 1 teaspoon salt and cook, stirring frequently, until al dente. Reserve ½ cup cooking water, then drain pasta and return it to pot. Add remaining ¼ teaspoon garlic, lemon zest and juice, reserved garlic-oil mixture, and reserved cooking water to pasta in pot. Stir until pasta is well coated with oil and no water remains in bottom of pot. Add basil, Parmesan, and pine nuts and toss to combine. Season with salt and pepper to taste. Serve, passing extra Parmesan separately.

variation

garlicky spaghetti with green olives and almonds
Omit lemon zest and reduce lemon juice to 1½ teaspoons. Stir ½ cup green olives, chopped fine, into pasta with lemon juice. Substitute Pecorino Romano for Parmesan and toasted sliced almonds for pine nuts.

pasta with roasted cauliflower, garlic, and walnuts

why this recipe works For a meatless yet substantial one-dish meal, we wanted to combine sweet, nutty roasted cauliflower with pasta and cheese, united by a simple sauce. Cutting the cauliflower into small pieces and sprinkling it with sugar maximized caramelization, and cooking it on a pre-heated baking sheet significantly reduced the roasting time. Roasted garlic turned out to be a key ingredient in our sauce; mashed with a little extra-virgin olive oil and lemon juice, it created a creamy puree with an earthy sweetness. Parsley, toasted walnuts, and Parmesan provided additional layers of flavor. Other pasta shapes can be substituted for the campanelle; however, their cup measurements may vary. Note that the garlic will still be in the oven when you add the cauliflower to the hot baking sheet.

serves 2
total time: 1 hour 15 minutes

1 head garlic, outer papery skins removed and top quarter of head cut off and discarded

½ teaspoon plus 3 tablespoons extra-virgin olive oil

1 tablespoon lemon juice, plus extra for seasoning

⅛ teaspoon red pepper flakes

½ head cauliflower (1 pound), cored and cut into 1-inch florets

Salt and pepper

⅛ teaspoon sugar

6 ounces (2 cups) campanelle

¼ cup grated Parmesan cheese, plus extra for serving

2 teaspoons minced fresh parsley

2 tablespoons chopped walnuts, toasted

1. Adjust oven racks to middle and lower-middle positions and heat oven to 500 degrees. Place garlic head, cut side up, in center of 12-inch square of aluminum foil. Drizzle ½ teaspoon oil over garlic and wrap securely. Place packet on lower rack and place rimmed baking sheet on upper rack. Roast garlic for 35 minutes. Transfer packet to cutting board, let cool for 10 minutes, then unwrap garlic. Gently squeeze to remove cloves from skin, transfer cloves to small bowl, and mash smooth with fork. Stir in lemon juice and pepper flakes, then slowly whisk in 2 tablespoons oil.

2. While garlic roasts, toss cauliflower, remaining 1 tablespoon oil, ½ teaspoon salt, ⅛ teaspoon pepper, and sugar together in large bowl. Working quickly, carefully arrange cauliflower in single layer on hot baking sheet. Roast cauliflower until well browned and tender, 10 to 15 minutes, stirring halfway through roasting. Transfer cauliflower to cutting board, let cool slightly, and chop into ½-inch pieces.

3. Meanwhile, bring 4 quarts water to boil in large pot. Add pasta and 1 tablespoon salt and cook, stirring often, until al dente. Reserve ½ cup cooking water, then drain pasta and return it to pot. Add garlic mixture, chopped cauliflower, 2 tablespoons reserved cooking water, Parmesan, and parsley and toss to combine. Adjust consistency with remaining reserved cooking water as needed and season with salt, pepper, and extra lemon juice to taste. Sprinkle individual portions with walnuts. Serve, passing extra Parmesan separately.

soba noodles with roasted eggplant and sesame

why this recipe works With their unique flavor and chewy texture, Japanese soba noodles require little adornment, so we knew they would make a quick and substantial meal for two. The creamy texture and mild flavor of cooked eggplant was the perfect foil for the rich, nutty noodles. Roasting proved an easy, hands-off way to cook the eggplant, and tossing it with soy sauce beforehand helped season the vegetable and draw out its moisture. A combination of soy sauce, oyster sauce, Asian chili-garlic sauce, sake, and toasted sesame oil formed a bold, complex sauce that provided a nice balance of sweet and spicy flavors. A garnish of toasted sesame seeds was the perfect finishing touch. Do not substitute other types of noodles for the soba noodles here.

serves 2
total time: 50 minutes

2 tablespoons vegetable oil

1 pound eggplant, cut into 1-inch pieces

2 tablespoons soy sauce

2 tablespoons sugar

1 tablespoon oyster sauce

1 tablespoon toasted sesame oil

1½ teaspoons Asian chili-garlic sauce

2 teaspoons sake or dry vermouth

4 ounces soba noodles

¼ cup fresh cilantro leaves

1 teaspoon sesame seeds, toasted

1. Adjust oven rack to middle position and heat oven to 450 degrees. Line rimmed baking sheet with aluminum foil and brush with 1½ teaspoons vegetable oil. Toss eggplant with remaining 1½ tablespoons vegetable oil and 1½ teaspoons soy sauce, then spread on prepared sheet. Roast until well browned and tender, 25 to 30 minutes, stirring halfway through roasting.

2. In small saucepan, whisk remaining 1½ tablespoons soy sauce, sugar, oyster sauce, sesame oil, chili-garlic sauce, and sake together. Cook over medium heat until sugar has dissolved, about 1 minute; cover and set aside.

3. Meanwhile, bring 4 quarts water to boil in large pot. Add noodles and cook, stirring often, until tender. Reserve ½ cup cooking water, then drain noodles and return them to pot. Add roasted eggplant, sauce, and cilantro and toss to combine. Adjust consistency with reserved cooking water as needed. Sprinkle individual portions with sesame seeds. Serve.

potato gnocchi with brown butter–sage sauce

why this recipe works Making gnocchi from scratch is a labor of love that is well worth the time, whether it's for a special occasion or you simply want to make this restaurant favorite as a weekend project. But many recipes churn out dozens of dumplings, so we aimed to make a batch perfectly scaled for two. We started by parcooking the potatoes in the microwave before baking them in the oven. After peeling them, we put the cooked potatoes through a ricer, which eliminated lumps. An egg, while not traditional, tenderized our gnocchi. Transferring the cooked gnocchi directly into the skillet with a nutty brown butter–sage sauce ensured that all gnocchi were thoroughly napped in buttery goodness—and as a bonus, the starch from the gnocchi added body to the sauce. For the most accurate measurements, weigh the potatoes and flour. After processing and measuring, you may have extra potatoes; discard any extra or set aside for another use.

serves 2
total time: 1 hour 20 minutes

gnocchi
2 pounds russet potatoes, unpeeled

1 large egg, lightly beaten

¾ cup plus 1 tablespoon (4 ounces) all-purpose flour

Salt

sauce
4 tablespoons unsalted butter, cut into 4 pieces

1 small shallot, minced

1 teaspoon minced fresh sage

1½ teaspoons lemon juice

¼ teaspoon salt

1. for the gnocchi Adjust oven rack to middle position and heat oven to 450 degrees. Poke each potato 8 times with paring knife. Microwave potatoes until slightly softened at ends, about 10 minutes, flipping potatoes halfway through cooking. Transfer potatoes directly to oven rack and bake until skewer glides easily through flesh and potatoes yield to gentle pressure, 18 to 20 minutes.

2. Holding potatoes with dish towel, peel with paring knife. Process potatoes through ricer or food mill onto rimmed baking sheet. Gently spread potatoes into even layer and let cool for 5 minutes.

3. Transfer 3 cups (16 ounces) warm potatoes to bowl. Using fork, gently stir in egg until just combined. Sprinkle flour and 1 teaspoon salt over top and gently combine using fork until no pockets of dry flour remain. Press mixture into rough ball, transfer to lightly floured counter, and gently knead until smooth but slightly sticky, about 1 minute, lightly dusting counter with flour as needed to prevent sticking.

4. Line 2 clean rimmed baking sheets with parchment paper and dust liberally with flour. Divide dough into 8 equal pieces. Lightly dust counter with flour. Gently roll 1 piece of dough into ½-inch-thick rope, dusting with flour to prevent sticking. Cut rope into ¾-inch lengths.

5. Holding fork with tines upside down in 1 hand, press each dough piece, cut side down, against tines with thumb of other hand to create indentation. Roll dough down tines to form ridges on sides. If dough sticks, dust thumb and/or fork with flour. Transfer formed gnocchi to prepared sheets and repeat with remaining dough.

6. for the sauce Melt butter in 12-inch skillet over medium-high heat, swirling occasionally, until butter is browned and releases nutty aroma, about 1½ minutes. Off heat, stir in shallot and sage and cook using residual heat from skillet until fragrant, about 1 minute. Stir in lemon juice and salt. Cover to keep warm.

7. Bring 4 quarts water to boil in large pot. Add 1 tablespoon salt. Using parchment paper as sling, add half of gnocchi and cook until firm and just cooked through, about 90 seconds (gnocchi should float to surface after about 1 minute). Remove gnocchi with slotted spoon, transfer to skillet with sauce, and cover to keep warm. Repeat with remaining gnocchi and transfer to skillet. Gently toss gnocchi with sauce to combine, and serve.

baked manicotti

why this recipe works Well-made versions of this Italian-American classic, which features tender pasta tubes stuffed with rich ricotta filling and blanketed with tomato sauce, can be eminently satisfying. But when cooking for two, the hassle of putting it all together hardly seems worth it. Could we find a simpler, better method for making manicotti? Stuffing and baking raw pasta tubes proved problematic, but soaking no-boil lasagna noodles until just pliable and rolling them up around the filling worked perfectly—and saved us the trouble of cooking the pasta separately. To ensure our filling was thick and creamy—not thin and runny—we mixed ricotta with a generous amount of mozzarella. Finally, just six ingredients whirred in the food processor gave us a fresh, bright tomato sauce in no time. As the manicotti baked, the tomato sauce reduced just enough that it didn't taste raw and kept the manicotti moist and tender. Do not substitute fat-free ricotta cheese here.

serves 2
total time: 1 hour 20 minutes

sauce
1 (14.5-ounce) can diced tomatoes

1 tablespoon extra-virgin olive oil

2 garlic cloves, minced

¼ teaspoon salt

⅛ teaspoon red pepper flakes (optional)

1 tablespoon chopped fresh basil

filling and pasta
8 ounces (1 cup) whole-milk or part-skim ricotta cheese

3 ounces whole-milk mozzarella cheese, shredded (¾ cup)

2 ounces Parmesan cheese, grated (1 cup)

1 large egg, lightly beaten

1 tablespoon chopped fresh basil

¼ teaspoon salt

⅛ teaspoon pepper

6 no-boil lasagna noodles

1. for the sauce Adjust oven rack to middle position and heat oven to 400 degrees. Process tomatoes and their juice, olive oil, garlic, salt, and pepper flakes, if using, in food processor until smooth, about 10 seconds. Transfer mixture to bowl and stir in basil.

2. for the filling and pasta Combine ricotta, mozzarella, ½ cup Parmesan, egg, basil, salt, and pepper in bowl.

3. Fill large bowl halfway with boiling water. Slip noodles into water, one at a time. Let noodles soak until pliable, about 5 minutes, separating noodles with tip of knife to prevent sticking. Remove noodles from water and place in single layer on clean dish towels.

4. Spread ½ cup sauce over bottom of 8½ by 4½-inch loaf pan. Transfer noodles to counter with short sides facing you. Spread ¼ cup ricotta mixture evenly over bottom three-quarters of each noodle. Roll noodles up around filling and lay them, seam side down, in pan. Spoon remaining sauce over top to cover noodles completely. Sprinkle with remaining ½ cup Parmesan.

5. Cover pan tightly with aluminum foil and bake until bubbling, about 25 minutes. Remove foil and continue to bake until cheese is browned in spots, about 10 minutes. Let cool for 15 minutes before serving.

skillet eggplant parmesan

why this recipe works Eggplant Parmesan typically involves a large, satisfying casserole meant to serve a crowd. But it is notoriously tedious to make and often seems out of the question for just two. Enter skillet eggplant Parmesan. We reinvented this comfort food classic so we could make it in a fraction of the time. To start, we skipped the step of slowly simmering the tomato sauce and made a simple one in the food processor—no cooking required. To quickly prepare our eggplant slices, we tossed them with flour in a zipper-lock bag and then dipped them in beaten egg and coated them in a savory mixture of homemade bread crumbs mixed with a hefty ¾ cup of grated Parmesan cheese. After frying the eggplant in batches, we assembled our skillet casserole with sauce, circles of fried eggplant, more sauce, and a topping of cheese. Just 15 minutes in a hot oven and our generously sized eggplant Parmesan for two was ready to serve. Be sure to leave the outer edges of the eggplant slices unsauced in step 5 so that they remain crisp once baked.

serves 2
total time: 1 hour

tomato sauce
1 (14.5-ounce) can whole peeled tomatoes, drained with juice reserved

1 tablespoon extra-virgin olive oil

1 garlic clove, minced

¼ teaspoon salt

eggplant
4 slices high-quality white sandwich bread, torn into quarters

1½ ounces Parmesan cheese, grated (¾ cup)

Salt and pepper

2 large eggs

½ cup unbleached all-purpose flour

1 small globe eggplant (about 12 ounces), sliced into ¼-inch-thick rounds

½ cup vegetable oil

4 ounces mozzarella cheese, shredded (1 cup)

¼ cup chopped fresh basil (optional)

1. for the tomato sauce Process tomatoes, olive oil, garlic, and salt together in food processor until pureed, about 15 seconds. Transfer mixture to liquid measuring cup, and add reserved tomato juice as needed until sauce measures 1½ cups. (Wash and dry bowl of food processor before making bread crumbs.)

2. for the eggplant Adjust oven rack to lower-middle position and heat oven to 425 degrees. Pulse bread in food processor to fine, even crumbs, about 15 pulses (you should have about 4 cups). Transfer crumbs to pie plate and stir in ½ cup Parmesan, ¼ teaspoon salt, and ¼ teaspoon pepper. Beat eggs in second pie plate. Combine flour and ½ teaspoon pepper in large zipper-lock bag.

3. Place eggplant slices in bag of flour, shake bag to coat eggplant, then remove eggplant from bag and shake off excess flour. Using tongs, coat floured eggplant with egg mixture, allowing excess to drip off. Coat all sides of eggplant with bread crumbs, pressing on

crumbs to help them adhere. Lay breaded eggplant slices on wire rack set over rimmed baking sheet.

4. Heat oil in 12-inch ovensafe nonstick skillet over medium-high heat until shimmering. Add half of breaded eggplant slices to skillet and cook until well browned on both sides, about 4 minutes, flipping them halfway through cooking. Transfer eggplant to wire rack and repeat with remaining breaded eggplant.

5. Pour off oil left in skillet and wipe out skillet with wad of paper towels. Spread 1 cup of tomato sauce over bottom of skillet. Layer eggplant slices evenly into skillet, overlapping them slightly. Dollop remaining ½ cup sauce on top of eggplant and sprinkle with remaining ¼ cup Parmesan and mozzarella, leaving outer 1 inch of eggplant slices clean.

6. Transfer skillet to oven and bake until bubbling and cheese is browned, 13 to 15 minutes. Let eggplant cool for 5 minutes, then sprinkle with basil (if using) and serve.

easy skillet cheese pizza

why this recipe works Making pizza from scratch can be a bit of a production, so with only two to feed it's not surprising that takeout trumps homemade. But with this perfectly scaled and easy-to-make dough, a no-cook sauce, and a method that uses a skillet, there's really no excuse not to make it yourself. First we oiled our skillet to prevent sticking and to encourage browning. We then added the dough and topped it with a sauce of diced tomatoes, olive oil, and garlic; this simple sauce plus a combination of mozzarella and a little Parmesan were all the toppings this easy pizza needed. After giving our assembled pizza a jump start on the stovetop, we transferred the skillet to the oven to allow it to finish cooking through, until the cheese melted and the crust turned brown. You can substitute 8 ounces of store-bought pizza dough for the dough in this recipe. Let the dough sit at room temperature while preparing the remaining ingredients and heating the oven; otherwise, it will be difficult to stretch. Feel free to add simple toppings before baking, but keep the toppings light or they may weigh down the thin crust and make it soggy.

3 tablespoons extra-virgin olive oil

½ cup canned diced tomatoes, drained with juice reserved

1 small garlic clove, minced

⅛ teaspoon salt

1 recipe Basic Pizza Dough, room temperature

4 ounces whole-milk mozzarella cheese, shredded (1 cup)

2 tablespoons grated Parmesan cheese

1. Adjust oven rack to upper-middle position and heat oven to 500 degrees. Grease 12-inch oven-safe skillet with 2 tablespoons oil.

2. Pulse tomatoes, garlic, salt, and remaining 1 tablespoon oil together in food processor until coarsely ground, about 12 pulses. Transfer mixture to liquid measuring cup and add reserved tomato juice until sauce measures ½ cup.

3. Place dough on lightly floured counter. Press and roll dough into 11-inch round. Transfer dough to prepared skillet; reshape as needed. Spread sauce over dough, leaving ½-inch border at edge. Sprinkle mozzarella and Parmesan evenly over sauce.

4. Set skillet over high heat and cook until outside edge of dough is set, pizza is lightly puffed, and bottom crust is spotty brown when gently lifted with spatula, about 3 minutes.

5. Transfer pizza to oven and bake until crust is brown and cheese is golden in spots, 7 to 10 minutes. Using potholders (skillet handle will be hot), remove skillet from oven and slide pizza onto cutting board. Let pizza cool for 5 minutes before slicing and serving.

serves 2
total time: 1 hour 30 minutes

basic pizza dough
makes 8 ounces dough
All-purpose flour can be substituted for the bread flour, but the resulting crust will be less chewy. You can slow down the dough's rising time by letting it rise in the refrigerator for 8 to 16 hours in step 2; let the refrigerated dough soften at room temperature for 30 minutes before using.

1 cup (5½ ounces) bread flour, plus extra as needed

¾ teaspoon instant or rapid-rise yeast

½ teaspoon salt

1½ teaspoons olive oil

7 tablespoons warm water (110 degrees)

1. Process flour, yeast, and salt in food processor until combined, about 2 seconds. With processor running, slowly add oil, then water, and process until dough forms sticky ball that clears sides of bowl, 1½ to 2 minutes. (If, after 1 minute, dough is sticky and clings to blade, add extra flour, 1 tablespoon at a time, as needed until it clears sides of bowl.)

2. Transfer dough to lightly floured counter and shape into tight ball. Place dough in large, lightly oiled bowl and cover tightly with greased plastic wrap. Let rise at room temperature until doubled in size, 1 to 1½ hours.

variation
whole-wheat pizza dough
Substitute ½ cup whole-wheat flour for ½ cup of bread flour.

asian braised tofu with butternut squash and eggplant

why this recipe works Braising is a great method for preparing tofu, as the tofu readily soaks up all the flavors of the braising liquid as it cooks. We decided to use rich, creamy coconut milk as the base of an Asian-inspired braise. Sautéed onion, garlic, ginger, and lemon grass provided a bold aromatic foundation for our sauce. Cutting the tofu into cubes increased its surface area, allowing it to absorb maximum flavor. To round out the dish, we wanted a couple of hearty, earthy vegetables that would benefit from a quick braise: Sweet, creamy butternut squash and meaty eggplant won tasters over. To deepen their flavors, we browned them in the pan before adding the tofu and braising liquid. If using prepeeled and seeded squash from the supermarket, you will need 8 ounces for this recipe. The tofu and vegetables are delicate and can break apart easily, so be gentle when stirring. Serve with Simple White Rice (page 164).

serves 2
total time: 1 hour

14 ounces extra-firm tofu, cut into ¾-inch pieces

1 tablespoon vegetable oil

1 pound butternut squash, peeled, seeded, and cut into ½-inch pieces (1½ cups)

½ eggplant (8 ounces), cut into ½-inch pieces

1 small onion, chopped fine

4 garlic cloves, minced

1 tablespoon grated fresh ginger

1 lemon grass stalk, trimmed to bottom 6 inches and bruised with back of knife

¾ cup vegetable broth

½ cup canned light coconut milk

2 teaspoons soy sauce

¼ cup minced fresh cilantro

2 teaspoons lime juice

Salt and pepper

1. Line baking sheet with triple layer of paper towels. Spread tofu over prepared sheet and let drain for 15 minutes.

2. Meanwhile, heat 1 teaspoon oil in 10-inch nonstick skillet over medium-high heat until shimmering. Add squash and cook until spotty brown and tender, 7 to 10 minutes; transfer to bowl. Return now-empty skillet to medium-high heat, add 1 teaspoon oil, and heat until shimmering. Add eggplant and cook until golden brown, 5 to 7 minutes; transfer to bowl with squash.

3. Heat remaining 1 teaspoon oil in again-empty skillet over medium heat until shimmering. Add onion and cook until softened and lightly browned, 5 to 7 minutes. Stir in garlic, ginger, and lemon grass and cook until fragrant, about 30 seconds. Gently stir in tofu, broth, coconut milk, soy sauce, and cooked vegetables and bring to simmer. Reduce heat to medium-low, cover, and cook, stirring occasionally, until vegetables are softened, about 10 minutes. Uncover and continue to simmer until sauce is slightly thickened, about 2 minutes.

4. Off heat, discard lemon grass. Stir in cilantro and lime juice and season with salt and pepper to taste. Serve.

stuffed acorn squash with barley

why this recipe works For a vegetarian entrée that would satisfy even an ardent carnivore, we turned to stuffed squash. A single acorn squash, split in half and stuffed, was just right for two servings. Stuffing the raw squash and then roasting it gave us undercooked squash and dry filling, so we roasted the squash on its own first. We tried various grains in the filling and rustic, hearty barley was the clear favorite; we simply boiled it like pasta until it was tender. For fresh crunch and rich flavor, we added sautéed fennel, shallot, garlic, coriander, thyme, Parmesan, and pine nuts. But while our filling tasted great, it was a little dry and crumbly. To solve this problem, we scooped out the moist, tender roasted squash, mixed it with the filling, and mounded it all into the squash shells for a great texture and an attractive presentation. Make sure to use pearl barley, not hulled barley, here.

serves 2
total time: 1 hour 10 minutes

1 acorn squash (1½ pounds), halved pole to pole and seeded

2 tablespoons extra-virgin olive oil

Salt and pepper

¼ cup pearl barley

½ fennel bulb, stalks discarded, bulb cored and chopped fine

1 shallot, minced

3 garlic cloves, minced

½ teaspoon ground coriander

¼ teaspoon minced fresh thyme or pinch dried

1½ ounces Parmesan cheese, grated (¾ cup)

2 tablespoons minced fresh parsley

2 tablespoons pine nuts, toasted

1 tablespoon unsalted butter

Balsamic vinegar

1. Adjust oven racks to upper-middle and lower-middle positions and heat oven to 400 degrees. Line rimmed baking sheet with aluminum foil and spray with vegetable oil spray.

2. Brush cut sides of squash with 1 tablespoon oil, season with salt and pepper, and lay, cut side down, on prepared sheet. Roast on lower rack until tender and tip of paring knife inserted into flesh meets no resistance, 45 to 55 minutes. Remove squash from oven and increase oven temperature to 450 degrees.

3. Meanwhile, bring 2 cups water to boil in small saucepan. Stir in barley and ¼ teaspoon salt and cook until barley is tender, 20 to 25 minutes; drain and set aside. Wipe saucepan clean.

4. Heat remaining 1 tablespoon oil in now-empty saucepan over medium heat until shimmering. Add fennel and shallot and cook until softened and lightly browned, 5 to 7 minutes. Stir in garlic, coriander, and thyme and cook until fragrant, about 30 seconds. Off heat, stir in cooked barley, ½ cup Parmesan, parsley, pine nuts, and butter. Season with salt and pepper to taste.

5. Flip roasted squash over and scoop out flesh, leaving ⅛-inch thickness of flesh in each shell. Gently fold cooked squash into barley mixture, then mound mixture evenly in squash shells. Sprinkle with remaining ¼ cup Parmesan and bake on upper rack until heated through and cheese is melted, 5 to 10 minutes. Drizzle with vinegar to taste and serve.

fennel, olive, and goat cheese tarts

why this recipe works We wanted to make elegant, savory tarts inspired by the flavors of the Mediterranean, and our goal was to keep it easy enough for a weeknight dinner. For the base, we reached for convenient store-bought puff pastry. Fresh, anise-flavored fennel and briny cured olives made a light but flavorful combination for the filling. Tangy goat cheese brightened with fresh basil contrasted nicely with the rich, flaky pastry and helped bind the vegetables and pastry together. Parbaking the pastry without the weight of the filling allowed it to puff up nicely. To keep the filling firmly in place, we cut a border around the edges of the baked crusts and lightly pressed down the centers to make neat beds for the cheese and vegetables. Just 5 minutes more in the oven heated the filling through and browned the crusts beautifully. To thaw frozen puff pastry, let it sit either in the refrigerator for 24 hours or on the counter for 30 minutes to 1 hour.

serves 2
total time: 50 minutes

½ (9½ by 9-inch) sheet puff pastry, thawed

4 ounces goat cheese, softened

¼ cup chopped fresh basil

1½ tablespoons extra-virgin olive oil

½ teaspoon grated lemon zest plus 2 teaspoons juice

Salt and pepper

½ fennel bulb, stalks discarded, bulb cored and sliced thin

1 garlic clove, minced

¼ cup dry white wine

¼ cup pitted oil-cured black olives, chopped

1. Adjust oven rack to middle position and heat oven to 425 degrees. Line baking sheet with parchment paper. Cut pastry sheet in half widthwise to make 2 squares and lay on prepared sheet. Poke pastry squares all over with fork and bake until puffed and golden brown, 12 to 15 minutes, rotating sheet halfway through baking. Using tip of paring knife, cut ½-inch-wide border into top of each pastry shell, then press centers down with your fingertips.

2. While pastry bakes, mix goat cheese, 2 tablespoons basil, 2 teaspoons oil, lemon zest, and ¼ teaspoon pepper together in small bowl. Heat remaining 2½ teaspoons oil in 8-inch skillet over medium heat until shimmering. Add fennel and cook until softened and lightly browned, about 5 to 7 minutes. Stir in garlic and cook until fragrant, about 30 seconds. Stir in wine, scraping up any browned bits, cover, and cook for 5 minutes. Uncover and continue to cook until liquid has evaporated and fennel is very soft, 3 to 5 minutes. Off heat, stir in lemon juice and olives.

3. Spread goat cheese mixture evenly over centers of prebaked tart shells, leaving raised edges clean, then spoon fennel mixture evenly over cheese layer. Transfer filled tarts to oven and bake until cheese is heated through and crust is deep golden brown, about 5 minutes. Sprinkle with remaining 2 tablespoons basil and season with salt and pepper to taste. Serve.

asparagus and goat cheese frittata

why this recipe works Breakfast for dinner can be a fun way to switch things up, and a well-seasoned, savory frittata made with bold ingredients makes for a substantial, pantry-friendly meal. To ensure that our frittata was cohesive, we chopped the filling ingredients small so that they could be evenly incorporated into the eggs. To help the eggs stay tender even when cooked at a relatively high temperature, we added milk and salt. The liquid diluted the proteins, making it harder for them to coagulate and turn the eggs rubbery, while salt weakened the interactions between proteins, producing a softer curd. Finally, for eggs that were cooked fully and evenly, we started the frittata on the stovetop, stirring until a spatula left a trail in the curds, and then transferred the skillet to the oven to gently finish. This recipe works best with thin and medium-size asparagus spears. This frittata can also be served warm or at room temperature. Serve with a Basic Green Salad (page 169).

serves 2
total time: 30 minutes

6 large eggs

2 tablespoons whole milk

Salt and pepper

1½ teaspoons extra-virgin olive oil

8 ounces asparagus, trimmed and cut into ¼-inch lengths

¼ teaspoon grated lemon zest plus ¼ teaspoon juice

2 ounces goat cheese, crumbled into ½-inch pieces (½ cup)

1 tablespoon chopped fresh mint

1. Adjust oven rack to middle position and heat oven to 350 degrees. Whisk eggs, milk, and ¼ teaspoon salt in bowl until well combined.

2. Heat oil in 8-inch ovensafe nonstick skillet over medium-high heat until shimmering. Add asparagus, lemon zest and juice, ⅛ teaspoon salt, and ⅛ teaspoon pepper; cook, stirring frequently, until asparagus is crisp-tender, 3 to 4 minutes.

3. Add goat cheese, mint, and egg mixture and cook, using rubber spatula to stir and scrape bottom of skillet until large curds form and spatula leaves trail through eggs but eggs are still very wet, 30 seconds. Smooth curds into even layer and cook, without stirring, for 30 seconds. Transfer skillet to oven and bake until frittata is slightly puffy and surface bounces back when lightly pressed, 6 to 9 minutes. Using rubber spatula, loosen frittata from skillet and transfer to cutting board. Let stand for 5 minutes before slicing and serving.

skillet summer vegetable tamale pie

why this recipe works Packed with summery zucchini, fresh corn, and poblano chile and bound in a cheesy tomato sauce, this one-dish skillet supper for two is as filling as it is easy to make. The poblano chile plus pepper Jack cheese and chili powder created a Southwestern flavor profile. We packed the vegetables into an 8-inch skillet, keeping the generous filling from spilling over. A layer of simple buttermilk cornbread spread on top and baked until golden brown provided a delicious foil for the saucy, spicy vegetables. If you don't have buttermilk on hand, you can substitute ⅓ cup of milk and 1½ teaspoons of lemon juice; stir together and let the mixture sit until it thickens, about 5 minutes. To make individual portions, divide the filling evenly between two 6-inch pie plates in step 4; spread half of the cornbread topping evenly over the filling in each pie plate and bake on a rimmed baking sheet. Serve with sour cream, if desired.

serves 2
total time: 50 minutes

filling
1 tablespoon extra-virgin olive oil

1 poblano chile, stemmed, seeded, and cut into ½-inch pieces

1 shallot, chopped

Salt and pepper

1 ear corn, kernels cut from cob

1 zucchini (8 ounces), quartered lengthwise and cut into ½-inch pieces

1 (14.5-ounce) can diced tomatoes, drained with juice reserved

1 teaspoon chili powder

2 ounces pepper Jack cheese, shredded (½ cup)

2 tablespoons chopped fresh cilantro

topping
⅓ cup (1⅔ ounces) all-purpose flour

⅓ cup (1⅔ ounces) cornmeal

1 tablespoon sugar

¼ teaspoon baking powder

⅛ teaspoon baking soda

¼ teaspoon salt

⅓ cup buttermilk

1 large egg

1 tablespoon unsalted butter, melted and cooled

1. for the filling Adjust oven rack to middle position and heat oven to 450 degrees. Heat oil in 8-inch ovensafe skillet over medium heat until shimmering. Add poblano, shallot, and ¼ teaspoon salt and cook, stirring frequently, until softened, about 5 minutes. Add corn, zucchini, and tomatoes. Cover and cook, stirring occasionally, until just tender, 6 to 8 minutes. Stir in chili powder and cook until fragrant, about 30 seconds.

2. Off heat, stir in pepper Jack, cilantro, and reserved tomato juice. Season with salt and pepper to taste; set aside.

3. for the topping Whisk flour, cornmeal, sugar, baking powder, baking soda, and salt together in medium bowl. Whisk buttermilk and egg together in small bowl. Stir buttermilk mixture into flour mixture until uniform, then stir in melted butter until just combined.

4. Dollop cornbread topping evenly over filling, then spread into even layer, covering filling completely. Bake until cornbread is golden and toothpick inserted in center comes out clean, 12 to 15 minutes. Serve.

appendix

15 back-pocket sides

Even the most basic of dishes, such as rice or couscous, can be tricky to scale down for two with just the right ratio of liquid to rice or grain. We did the testing so you don't have to and compiled some of our favorite veggie, salad, and grain sides that will go with almost any main dish to help round out your meal.

simple white rice

serves 2

You will need a small saucepan (1 to 2 quarts) with a tight-fitting lid for this recipe. A nonstick saucepan will help prevent the rice from sticking.

1 teaspoon vegetable oil

¾ cup long-grain white, basmati, or jasmine rice, rinsed

1¼ cups water

¼ teaspoon salt

1. Heat oil in small saucepan over medium heat until shimmering. Stir in rice and cook until edges of grains begin to turn translucent, about 2 minutes. Stir in water and salt and bring to boil. Reduce heat to low, cover, and simmer until all liquid is absorbed, 18 to 22 minutes.

2. Remove saucepan from heat. Remove lid, place folded clean dish towel over saucepan, and replace lid. Let rice sit for 10 minutes, then gently fluff with fork. Serve.

classic rice pilaf

serves 2

Long-grain white rice can be substituted here. You will need a small saucepan (1 to 2 quarts) with a tight-fitting lid for this recipe. A nonstick saucepan will help prevent the rice from sticking. For an accurate measurement of boiling water, bring a full kettle of water to a boil, then measure out the desired amount.

1 tablespoon unsalted butter or olive oil

1 small shallot, minced

¾ cup basmati rice, rinsed

1¼ cups boiling water

¼ teaspoon salt

⅛ teaspoon pepper

1. Melt butter in small saucepan over medium heat. Add shallot and cook until softened, about 2 minutes. Stir in rice and cook until edges of grains begin to turn translucent, about 2 minutes. Stir in boiling water, salt, and pepper and bring back to boil. Reduce heat to low, cover, and simmer until all liquid is absorbed, 12 to 15 minutes.

2. Remove saucepan from heat. Remove lid, place folded clean dish towel over saucepan, and replace lid. Let rice sit for 10 minutes, then gently fluff with fork. Serve.

hands-off baked brown rice

serves 2

The test kitchen's preferred loaf pan measures 8½ by 4½ inches; if you use a 9 by 5-inch loaf pan, start checking for doneness 5 minutes early. For an accurate measurement of boiling water, bring a full kettle of water to a boil, then measure out the desired amount.

1¼ cups boiling water

¾ cup long-grain, medium-grain, or short-grain brown rice, rinsed

2 teaspoons olive oil

Salt and pepper

1. Adjust oven rack to middle position and heat oven to 375 degrees. Combine boiling water, rice, oil, and ¼ teaspoon salt in 8½ by 4½-inch loaf pan. Cover pan tightly with double layer of aluminum foil. Bake until rice is tender and no water remains, 45 to 55 minutes.

2. Remove pan from oven and fluff rice with fork, scraping up any rice that has stuck to bottom. Cover pan with clean dish towel, then re-cover loosely with foil. Let rice sit for 10 minutes. Season with salt and pepper to taste and serve.

parmesan risotto

serves 2

The risotto will stiffen as it sits; loosen with hot broth or water.

2½ cups water

2 cups chicken broth

2 tablespoons unsalted butter

1 small onion, chopped fine

Salt and pepper

1 garlic clove, minced

¾ cup Arborio rice

½ cup dry white wine

1 ounce Parmesan cheese, grated (½ cup)

1. Bring water and broth to simmer in small saucepan over medium heat. Remove from heat, cover, and keep warm.

2. Melt 1 tablespoon butter in medium saucepan over medium-high heat. Add onion and ¼ teaspoon salt and cook until softened, about 5 minutes. Stir in garlic and cook until fragrant, about 30 seconds. Add rice and cook, stirring constantly, until grains are translucent around edges, about 1 minute. Add wine and cook, stirring frequently, until fully absorbed, 3 to 5 minutes.

3. Stir in 2 cups reserved warm broth. Reduce heat to medium-low, cover, and simmer until almost all liquid is absorbed, about 12 minutes.

4. Stir in ½ cup reserved warm broth and cook, stirring constantly, until absorbed, about 3 minutes. Repeat with additional broth 2 or 3 more times until rice is al dente (you may have broth left over). Off heat, stir in remaining 1 tablespoon butter and Parmesan. Season with salt and pepper to taste, and serve.

creamy parmesan polenta

serves 2

Be sure to use traditional dried polenta here, not instant polenta or precooked; dried polenta looks like coarse-ground cornmeal and can be found alongside cornmeal or pasta in the supermarket. It is important to cook the polenta over very low heat.

1⅔ cups water

Salt and pepper

Pinch baking soda

⅓ cup polenta

1 tablespoon unsalted butter

1 ounce Parmesan cheese, grated (½ cup), plus extra for serving

1. Bring water to boil in small saucepan over medium-high heat. Stir in ¼ teaspoon salt and baking soda. Slowly add polenta in steady stream, stirring constantly with wooden spoon or rubber spatula. Bring mixture to boil, stirring constantly, about 30 seconds. Reduce heat to lowest possible setting and cover.

2. After 5 minutes, whisk polenta to smooth out any lumps that may have formed, making sure to scrape down sides and bottom of saucepan. Cover and continue to cook, without stirring, until grains of cornmeal are tender but slightly al dente, 8 to 10 minutes longer. (Polenta should be loose and barely hold its shape; it will continue to thicken as it cools.)

3. Off heat, stir in butter and Parmesan and season with salt and pepper to taste. Cover and let sit for 5 minutes. Serve, passing extra Parmesan separately.

couscous with tomato, scallion, and lemon

serves 2

Do not use Israeli couscous in this recipe; its larger size requires a different cooking method. Whole-wheat couscous can be substituted for regular couscous.

⅓ cup couscous

1 tablespoon extra-virgin olive oil

1 shallot, minced

1 garlic clove, minced

¼ teaspoon grated lemon zest plus 1 teaspoon juice

Pinch cayenne pepper

¼ cup water

¼ cup chicken broth

1 plum tomato, cored, seeded, and chopped fine

½ scallion, sliced thin

Salt and pepper

1. Toast couscous in small sauce-pan over medium-high heat, stirring often, until some grains begin to brown, about 3 minutes. Transfer couscous to medium bowl.

2. Heat 1½ teaspoons oil in now-empty saucepan over medium heat until shimmering. Add shal-lot and cook until softened, about 2 minutes. Stir in garlic, lemon zest, and cayenne and cook until fragrant, about 30 seconds. Stir in water and broth and bring to boil.

3. Pour boiling liquid over cous-cous in bowl, cover bowl tightly with plastic wrap, and let sit until couscous is tender, about 12 min-utes. Uncover and fluff couscous with fork. Stir in remaining 1½ tea-spoons oil, lemon juice, tomato, and scallion. Season with salt and pepper to taste, and serve.

quinoa pilaf

serves 2

Placing a kitchen towel under the lid absorbs the steam, keeping the grains from getting soggy. If you buy unwashed quinoa (or if you are unsure whether it's washed), rinse it before cooking to remove its bitter protective coating (called saponin).

1 tablespoon extra-virgin olive oil

1 small onion, chopped fine

Salt and pepper

¾ cup quinoa

1¼ cups chicken broth

1 teaspoon minced fresh thyme or ¼ teaspoon dried

1. Heat oil in medium saucepan over medium-high heat until shimmering. Add onion and ¼ tea-spoon salt and cook until onion is softened, about 5 minutes.

2. Add quinoa and cook, stirring often, until quinoa is lightly toasted and aromatic, about 5 minutes. Stir in broth and thyme and bring to simmer. Reduce heat to low, cover, and simmer until quinoa is translucent and tender, 16 to 18 minutes.

3. Remove saucepan from heat. Remove lid, place folded clean kitchen towel over saucepan, and replace lid. Let quinoa sit for 10 minutes, then gently fluff with fork. Season with salt and pepper to taste, and serve.

mashed potatoes

serves 2

You can substitute whole milk for the half-and-half here, but the potatoes will taste a bit leaner. Make sure to cook the potatoes thoroughly; they are done if they break apart when a knife is inserted and gently wiggled.

1 pound Yukon Gold potatoes, peeled and sliced ½ inch thick

Salt and pepper

⅓ cup half-and-half, room temperature

3 tablespoons unsalted butter, melted and cooled

1. Place potatoes and 1 tablespoon salt in medium saucepan and add water to cover by 1 inch. Bring to boil over medium-high heat, then reduce to simmer and cook, stir-ring once or twice, until potatoes are tender, 12 to 15 minutes.

2. Drain potatoes and return to saucepan set on still-hot burner. Using potato masher, mash pota-toes until a few small lumps remain. Gently mix half-and-half and melted butter together in small bowl until combined. Add half-and-half mixture to potatoes and, using rubber spatula, fold gently to incorporate. Season with salt and pepper to taste, and serve immediately.

roasted red potatoes

serves 2

1 pound red potatoes, unpeeled, cut into ¾-inch wedges

1½ tablespoons extra-virgin olive oil

Salt and pepper

1. Adjust oven rack to middle position and heat oven to 425 degrees. Line rimmed baking sheet with aluminum foil. Toss potatoes with oil, ¼ teaspoon salt, and ⅛ teaspoon pepper and arrange cut side down in single layer on prepared sheet. Cover sheet tightly with foil and roast potatoes for 20 minutes.

2. Carefully remove top piece of foil and continue to roast, uncovered, until bottoms of potatoes are golden and crusty, 8 to 10 minutes. Remove sheet from oven and, using spatula, flip potatoes. Return sheet to oven and continue to roast potatoes until crusty and golden on second side, about 5 minutes. Season with salt and pepper to taste, and serve.

variation

roasted red potatoes with garlic and rosemary

Sprinkle potatoes with 1 tablespoon minced fresh rosemary during final 5 minutes of roasting in step 2. Toss roasted potatoes with 1 minced garlic clove before serving.

roasted sweet potatoes

serves 2

1 pound sweet potatoes, peeled, ends trimmed, and cut into ¾-inch-thick rounds

1 tablespoon vegetable oil

Salt and pepper

1. Line rimmed baking sheet with aluminum foil and spray with vegetable oil spray. Toss potatoes with oil until evenly coated, then season with salt and pepper. Arrange potatoes in single layer on prepared sheet and cover tightly with foil. Adjust oven rack to middle position and place potatoes in cold oven. Turn oven to 425 degrees and roast potatoes for 20 minutes.

2. Carefully remove top piece of foil and continue to roast, uncovered, until bottom edges of potatoes are golden brown, 8 to 10 minutes. Remove sheet from oven and, using spatula, carefully flip potatoes. Return sheet to oven and continue to roast until bottom edges of potatoes are golden brown, 8 to 10 minutes. Season with salt and pepper to taste, and serve.

sweet and tangy coleslaw

serves 2

If you don't have a salad spinner, use a colander to drain the cabbage and press out the residual liquid with a rubber spatula.

2 tablespoons cider vinegar, plus extra for seasoning

1 tablespoon vegetable oil

Pinch celery seeds

Salt and pepper

½ small head green cabbage, halved, cored, and shredded (4 cups)

2 tablespoons sugar, plus extra for seasoning

1 small carrot, peeled and shredded

1 tablespoon minced fresh parsley

1. Combine vinegar, oil, celery seeds, and pinch pepper in medium bowl. Place bowl in freezer until vinegar mixture is well chilled, at least 10 or up to 20 minutes.

2. While vinegar mixture chills, toss cabbage with sugar and ½ teaspoon salt in separate bowl. Cover and microwave until cabbage is partially wilted and reduced in volume by one-third, 45 to 90 seconds, stirring cabbage halfway through microwaving.

3. Transfer cabbage to salad spinner and spin until excess water is removed, 10 to 20 seconds. Add cabbage, carrot, and parsley to chilled vinegar and toss to combine. Season with extra vinegar, extra sugar, and salt to taste. Cover and refrigerate until chilled, at least 15 minutes or up to 24 hours. Toss to redistribute dressing and serve.

roasted brussels sprouts

serves 2

Look for Brussels sprouts that are about 1½ inches long; quarter sprouts longer than 2½ inches. Be careful not to cut off too much of the stem end when trimming the sprouts, or the leaves will fall away from the core.

8 ounces Brussels sprouts, trimmed and halved

4 teaspoons water

1 tablespoon olive oil

Salt and pepper

1. Adjust oven rack to upper-middle position and heat oven to 500 degrees. Toss Brussels sprouts with water, oil, ⅛ teaspoon salt, and pinch pepper and arrange cut side down in 12-inch ovensafe skillet.

2. Cover and roast sprouts for 10 minutes. Uncover and continue to roast until sprouts are well browned and tender, 10 to 12 minutes. Season with salt and pepper to taste, and serve.

roasted broccoli

serves 2

1 pound broccoli

2 tablespoons extra-virgin olive oil

¼ teaspoon sugar

¼ teaspoon salt

¼ teaspoon pepper

Lemon wedges

1. Adjust oven rack to lowest position, line rimmed baking sheet with aluminum foil, place sheet on rack, and heat oven to 500 degrees. Cut broccoli at juncture of florets and stalks and remove outer peel from stalk. Cut stalk into ½-inch-thick pieces. Cut crowns into 4 wedges if 3 to 4 inches in diameter, or into 6 wedges if 4 to 5 inches in diameter. Toss broccoli pieces with oil, sugar, salt, and pepper.

2. Carefully arrange broccoli flat side down in single layer on hot sheet and roast until stem pieces are well browned and tender and florets are lightly browned, 9 to 11 minutes. Serve with lemon wedges.

variation

roasted broccoli with olives, garlic, oregano, and lemon
While broccoli roasts, cook 1 tablespoon extra-virgin olive oil, 3 thinly sliced garlic cloves, and ¼ teaspoon red pepper flakes in 8-inch skillet over medium-low heat until garlic begins to brown, 5 to 7 minutes. Off heat, stir in 1 tablespoon chopped pitted kalamata olives, 1 teaspoon lemon juice, and ½ teaspoon minced fresh oregano. Toss roasted broccoli with olive mixture before serving.

cauliflower gratin

serves 2

You will need an 8½ by 5½-inch baking dish for this recipe.

½ cup panko bread crumbs

1½ teaspoons extra-virgin olive oil

10 ounces cauliflower florets, cut into 1-inch pieces

1 tablespoon water

½ (5.2-ounce) package Boursin Garlic and Fine Herbs cheese

¼ cup heavy cream

¼ teaspoon salt

⅛ teaspoon pepper

1. Adjust oven rack to middle position and heat oven to 450 degrees. Combine panko and oil in 8-inch nonstick skillet. Toast panko over medium-high heat, stirring often, until golden, about 3 minutes.

2. Meanwhile, microwave cauliflower and water together in covered bowl until tender, about 3 minutes; drain cauliflower.

3. Wipe bowl dry with paper towels. Microwave Boursin, cream, salt, and pepper in cleaned bowl until cheese is melted, about 1 minute. Whisk Boursin mixture until smooth, then add drained cauliflower and toss to coat.

4. Transfer cauliflower mixture to 8½ by 5½-inch baking dish and sprinkle with toasted panko. Bake until hot and lightly bubbling around edges, about 7 minutes. Transfer gratin to wire rack and let cool for 5 to 10 minutes before serving.

basic green salad

serves 2

Salads are an integral part of the dinner table, so it's helpful to know how to put together a basic, no-fuss bowl of greens. With so few components, it is important to use high-quality ingredients.

½ garlic clove, peeled

4 ounces (4 cups) lettuce, torn into bite-size pieces if necessary

Extra-virgin olive oil

Vinegar

Salt and pepper

Rub inside of salad bowl with garlic. Add lettuce. Holding thumb over mouth of olive oil bottle to control flow, slowly drizzle lettuce

with small amount of oil. Toss greens very gently. Continue to drizzle with oil and toss gently until greens are lightly coated and just glistening. Sprinkle with small amounts of vinegar, salt, and pepper to taste, and toss gently to coat. Serve.

classic vinaigrette

makes ¼ cup

This recipe yields enough to dress 8 to 10 cups of greens, so you'll have extra that you can store, which will save you time prepping your salad another day.

1 tablespoon wine vinegar

1½ teaspoons minced shallot

½ teaspoon mayonnaise

½ teaspoon Dijon mustard

⅛ teaspoon salt

Pinch pepper

3 tablespoons extra-virgin olive oil

Whisk vinegar, shallot, mayonnaise, mustard, salt, and pepper together in bowl until smooth. Whisking constantly, slowly drizzle in oil until emulsified. (Vinaigrette can be refrigerated for up to 2 weeks.)

brining chicken and pork

Brining chicken and pork involves soaking the raw meat in a saltwater solution before cooking. The brining solution flows into the meat, distributing moisture as well as seasoning the meat and protecting it from drying out. Brined meat retains more of its moisture as it cooks, resulting in juicier, more flavorful meat. We prefer to use table salt for brining since it dissolves quickly in water. Note that if you are buying pork that is enhanced (injected with a salt solution), it does not require brining

cut	water	table salt	time
poultry			
2 boneless, skinless chicken breasts	3 cups	1½ tablespoons	30 minutes to 1 hour
2 bone-in chicken breasts	1 quart	¼ cup	30 minutes to 1 hour
1½ pounds bone-in chicken pieces	1 quart	¼ cup	30 minutes to 1 hour
1 whole chicken	2 quarts	½ cup	1 hour
2 Cornish game hens	2 quarts	½ cup	30 minutes to 1 hour
pork			
12 ounces boneless country-style ribs	3 cups	1½ tablespoons	30 minutes to 1 hour
2 boneless pork chops	3 cups	1½ tablespoons	30 minutes to 1 hour
2 bone-in blade-cut pork chops	3 cups	1½ tablespoons	30 minutes to 1 hour
2 bone-in pork rib or center-cut chops	3 cups	1½ tablespoons	30 minutes to 1 hour
1 (12-ounce) pork tenderloin	1½ quarts	3 tablespoons	30 minutes to 1 hour

conversions and equivalents

Some say cooking is a science and an art. We would say that geography has a hand in it, too. Flours and sugars manufactured in the United Kingdom and elsewhere will feel and taste different from those manufactured in the United States. So we cannot promise that the pie crust you bake in Canada or England will taste the same as a pie crust baked in the States, but we can offer guidelines for converting weights and measures. We also recommend that you rely on your instincts when making our recipes. Refer to the visual cues provided. If the pie dough hasn't "come together," as described, you may need to add more water—even if the recipe doesn't tell you to. You be the judge.

The recipes in this book were developed using standard U.S. measures following U.S. government guidelines. The charts below offer equivalents for U.S. and metric measures. All conversions are approximate and have been rounded up or down to the nearest whole number. For example:

$$1 \text{ teaspoon } = 4.9292 \text{ milliliters, rounded up to 5 milliliters}$$
$$1 \text{ ounce } = 28.3495 \text{ grams, rounded down to 28 grams}$$

volume conversions

u.s.	metric
1 teaspoon	5 milliliters
2 teaspoons	10 milliliters
1 tablespoon	15 milliliters
2 tablespoons	30 milliliters
¼ cup	59 milliliters
⅓ cup	79 milliliters
½ cup	118 milliliters
¾ cup	177 milliliters
1 cup	237 milliliters
1¼ cups	296 milliliters
1½ cups	355 milliliters
2 cups (1 pint)	473 milliliters
2½ cups	591 milliliters
3 cups	710 milliliters
4 cups (1 quart)	0.946 liter
1.06 quarts	1 liter
4 quarts (1 gallon)	3.8 liters

weight conversions

ounces	grams
½	14
¾	21
1	28
1½	43
2	57
2½	71
3	85
3½	99
4	113
4½	128
5	142
6	170
7	198
8	227
9	255
10	283
12	340
16 (1 pound)	454

conversion for common baking ingredients

Baking is an exacting science. Because measuring by weight is far more accurate than measuring by volume, and thus more likely to produce reliable results, in our recipes we provide ounce measures in addition to cup measures for many ingredients. Refer to the chart below to convert these measures into grams.

ingredient	ounces	grams
flour		
1 cup all-purpose flour*	5	142
1 cup cake flour	4	113
1 cup whole-wheat flour	5½	156
sugar		
1 cup granulated (white) sugar	7	198
1 cup packed brown sugar (light or dark)	7	198
1 cup confectioners' sugar	4	113
cocoa powder		
1 cup cocoa powder	3	85
butter†		
4 tablespoons (½ stick, or ¼ cup)	2	57
8 tablespoons (1 stick, or ½ cup)	4	113
16 tablespoons (2 sticks, or 1 cup)	8	227

* *U.S. all-purpose flour, the most frequently used flour in this book, does not contain leaveners, as some European flours do. These leavened flours are called self-rising or self-raising. If you are using self-rising flour, take this into consideration before adding leavening to a recipe.*

† *In the United States, butter is sold both salted and unsalted. We generally recommend unsalted butter. If you are using salted butter, take this into consideration before adding salt to a recipe.*

oven temperatures

fahrenheit	celsius	gas mark
225	105	¼
250	120	½
275	135	1
300	150	2
325	165	3
350	180	4
375	190	5
400	200	6
425	220	7
450	230	8
475	245	9

converting temperatures from an instant-read thermometer

We include doneness temperatures in many of the recipes in this book. We recommend an instant-read thermometer for the job. Refer to the table at left to convert Fahrenheit degrees to Celsius. Or, for temperatures not represented in the chart, use this simple formula:

Subtract 32 degrees from the Fahrenheit reading, then divide the result by 1.8 to find the Celsius reading. For example: "Roast chicken until thighs register 175 degrees."

To convert
175°F − 32 = 143°
143° ÷ 1.8 = 79.44°C, rounded down to 79°C

index

Note: Page references in *italics* indicate photographs.